cply

William N. Copley
Selected Writings

Edited by Anthony Atlas
In cooperation with the William N. Copley Estate

Verlag der Buchhandlung Walther König

Contents

Editor's Note

This volume presents a useful companion for readers interested in the extraordinary life, work, and artistic milieu of William Nelson Copley (1919–1996). Though best known for his work as a painter, Copley was also a talented writer and it is through his writings—on art, artists, and his experiences—that we can better view his restless, colorful life. With the addition of interviews and correspondence, *Selected Writings* also affords critical insight into Copley's work and influences.

Prior to becoming a painter, Copley had tried his hand at fiction, working on a novel (the manuscript of which is now lost) based on his experiences during World War II. Shortly after, Copley was introduced to Surrealism through his brother-in-law, John Ployardt, and the two opened the Copley Galleries in Beverly Hills, which operated for six months in 1948–49. During this period, Copley abandoned fiction in favor of painting—his most cherished pursuit—although he didn't stop writing. While living in France, he wrote articles as a foreign correspondent for newspapers owned by the Copley Press, the company founded by his adoptive father, Ira Clifton Copley (1864–1947). Copley authored approximately 120 articles for the *San Diego Union*, *Evening Tribune*, and other Copley Press–owned newspapers in California and Illinois between 1951 and 1956. By the time he returned to the United States in 1963, he had divested himself of his shares in the family business and found success as an artist. With funds from his inheritance, he acquired a formidable collection of modern art and established himself as an important advocate for the Surrealists, whose work he collected passionately.

Copley's essays—on Serge Charchoune, Man Ray, and Marcel Duchamp, among others—saw print in such venues as *Art News*, *Art in America*, and the *New York Times*, and his formative prose ventures culminated in a brilliant short memoir, "Portrait of the Artist as a Young Dealer," first published in French translation in 1977, but written several years earlier. This hilarious, self-deprecating account made its English debut in an exhibition catalogue published in 1979 by Rice University, Houston, on the occasion of its Copley retrospective, *Reflection on a Past Life*. It is reprinted here in the book's opening section, Writings About Art and Artists, which presents Copley's writing about the artists dearest to him—in particular, Joseph Cornell, Marcel Duchamp, Francis Picabia, and Man Ray.

The second section, Interviews, Texts, and Letters, presents Copley's thoughts as CPLY, the artist. These pieces focus on the painterly aspects of his work and address his primary motivations as an artist: his concern with humor and satire, sexual politics, and the poetic and metaphorical dimensions of painting. Also included in this section is Copley's collection of satirical aphoristic statements, "Project for a Dictionary of Platitudes," which was the first of several texts Copley wrote in this style, and "Advice to a Young Artist," a series of supportive and thoughtful letters written to his friend Anne Doran.

In the third section, Early Writings, a selection of Copley's journalism is reprinted for the first time. In the 1950s, while living in Paris and nearby Longpont-sur-Orge, Copley wrote entertainingly on European life and culture for an American readership. Twelve of his articles are presented here, along with an uncredited report—now attributed to Copley—of Joseph Cornell's 1948 exhibition at the Copley Galleries. In engaging, conversational prose, Copley renders his encounters with Picasso in Vallauris, with Constantin Brancusi in the Impasse Ronsin—where Copley had his first Paris studio—and with such lesser-known figures as Bettina Yonick, an eye-catching opera singer, and Billy Beck, the "GI clown of Montparnasse." These brief dispatches are the earliest surviving examples of Copley's affable, affirming voice as a writer.

★

In the interest of readability, typographic errors and erratic punctuation present in the original sources have been silently corrected, but minor differences in spelling and capitalization, from piece to piece, have been retained. Each section of the book is sequenced chronologically according to date of composition when known; readers may refer to the Note on the Texts on p. 265 for more information. The Chronology on p. 253 outlines the primary events in Copley's life and provides biographical context for the texts included here.

It has been a privilege to work closely with the William N. Copley Estate on preparing this book. I am indebted to Billy Copley, Claire Copley, and Theo Yang Copley for their critical feedback and support, and for allowing extensive access to their father's archives. Claire's insight into her father's writing and her close involvement in shaping this book into its current form were crucial. Further gratitude is owed to publisher Walther König, whose relationship with Copley's work dates back to 1972, with the publication of Copley's artist's book *Notes on a Project for a Dictionary of Ridiculous Images*. Franz König, Hanna Schmandin, and Nicole Rankers at Verlag der Buchhandlung Walther König helped guide this project to completion. I am also grateful for the expertise and enthusiasm of colleagues at Kasmin gallery: Paul Kasmin, Nick Olney, Eric Gleason, Katharine Jaensch, Molly Taylor, Diego Flores, and Chris Stach. For their valued advice, I am thankful to Patty Brundage, Paul B. Franklin, Mark Nelson, and Vincent Fremont. Miles Champion was an invaluable copy editor and shared the heavy lifting during the last stage of the project, and much credit is due Becca Abbe, whose elegant book design perfectly complements the texts. For additional credits and acknowledgments, please see p. 270.

A.A.

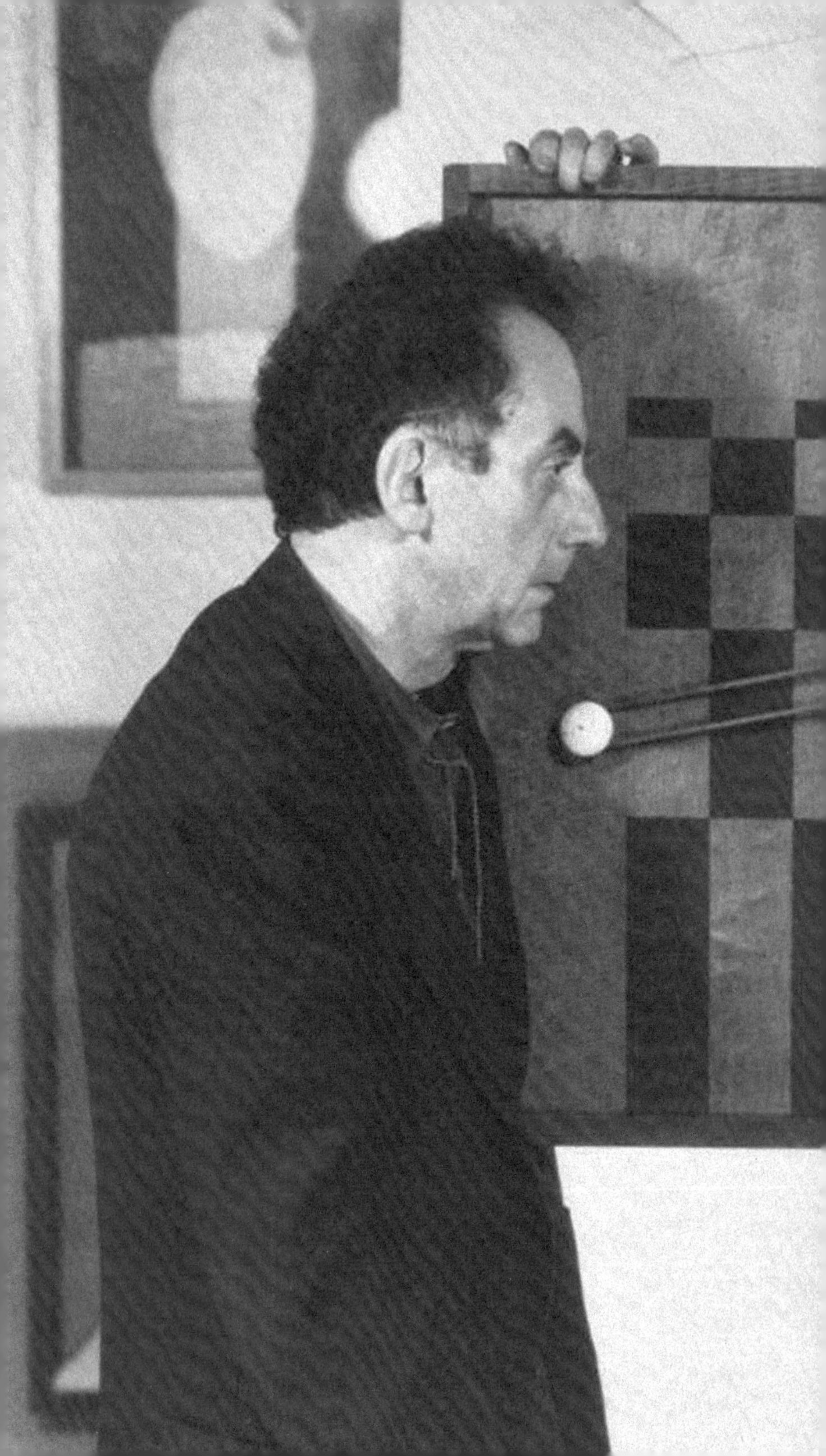

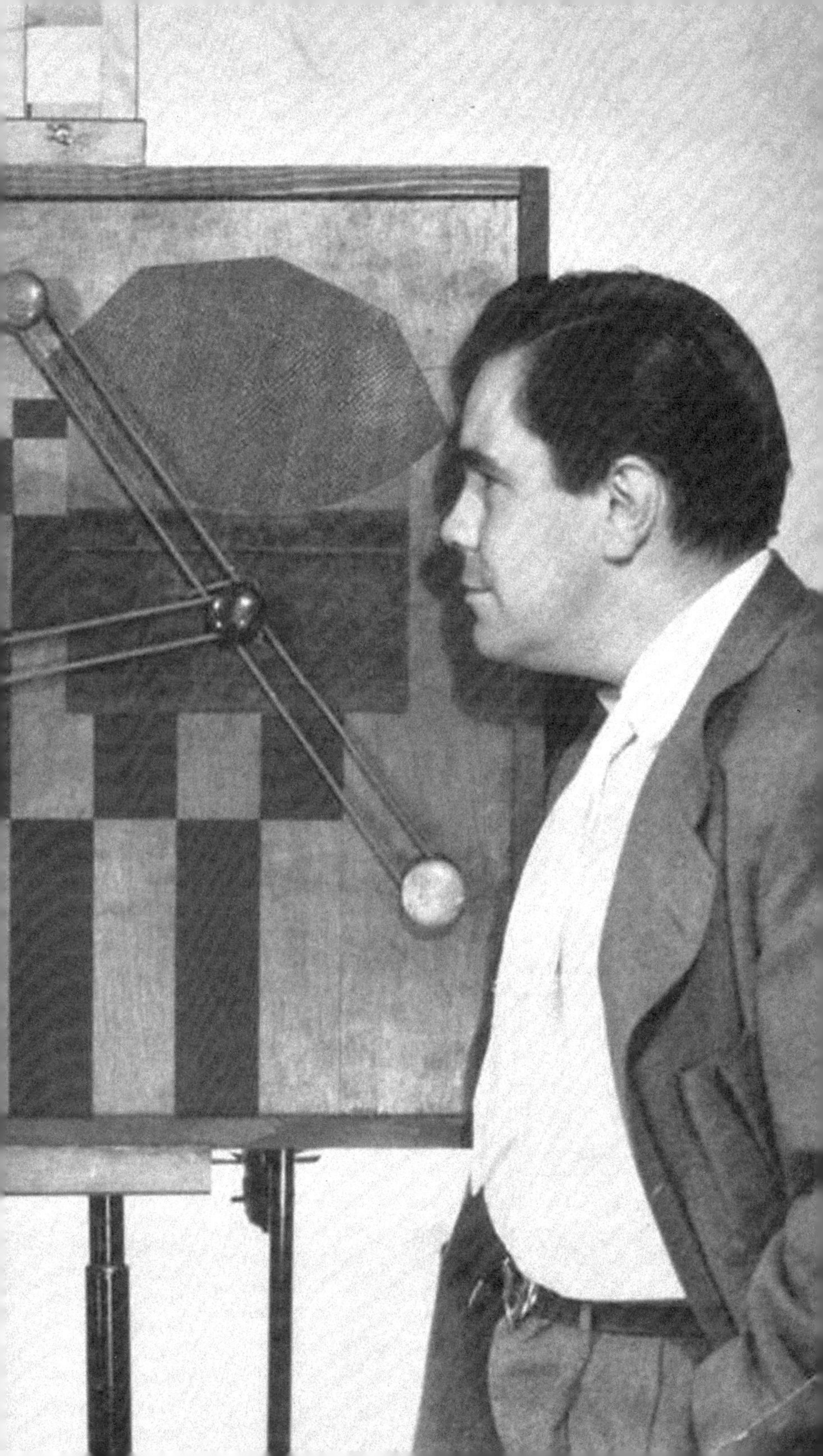

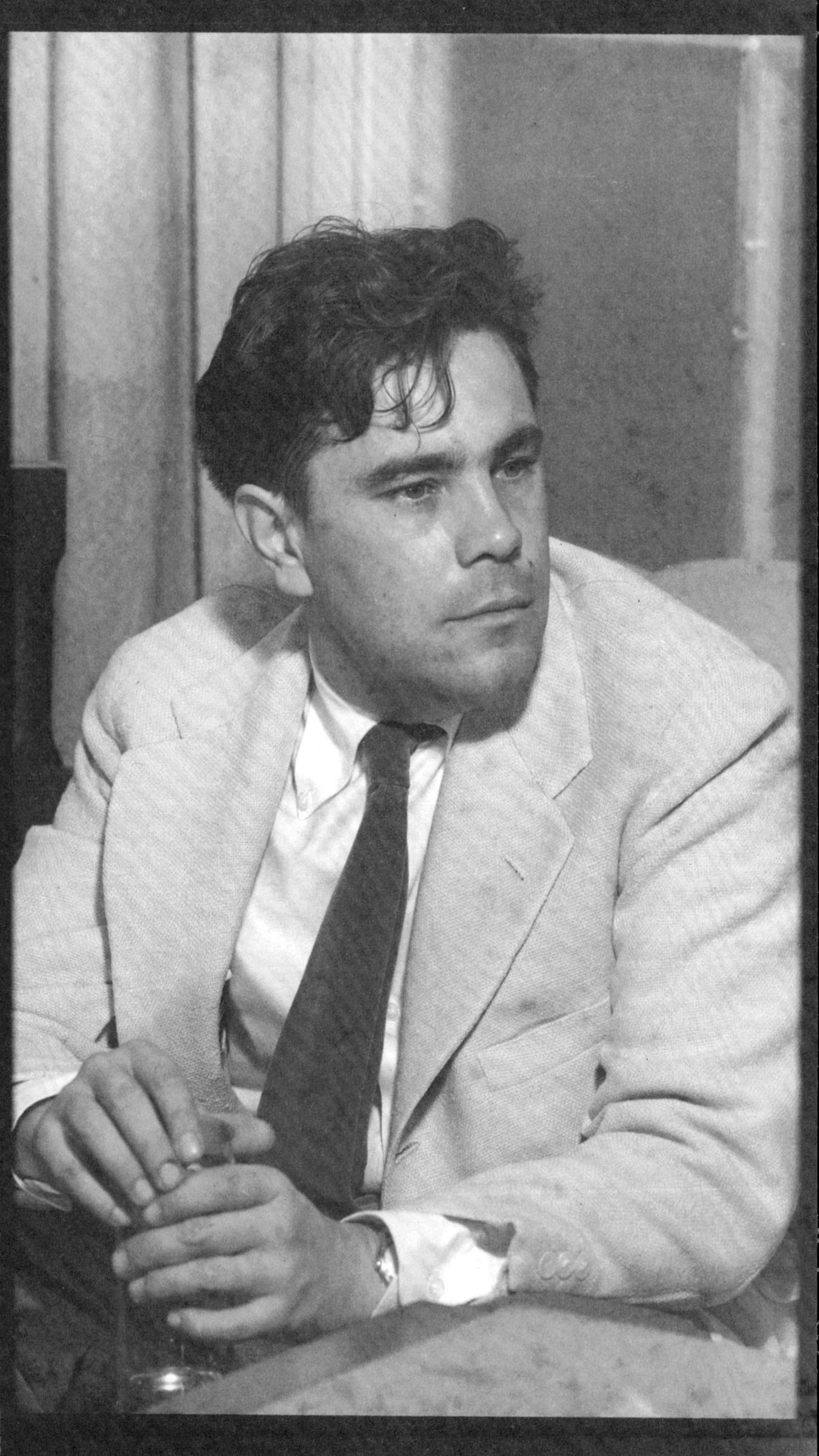

I. Writings About Art and Artists

Address by William N. Copley, Esq.

Opening remarks given at the Institute of Contemporary Arts, London, for An Exhibition Retrospective and Prospective of the Works of Man Ray, April 2, 1959

This exhibition is unusually timely. In a period during which Man (Kind, not Ray) has been confusing himself more and more, the contribution of Man Ray must be identified as a voice of clarity. (By clarity I mean that his painting defines concisely what art is and what it must be.)

During the lifetime of most of us here, what we call art has undergone a violent metamorphosis. It is really only now that we can properly evaluate the importance of the fact that Man Ray was on the scene during these upheavals.

I am going to risk Man Ray's displeasure in mentioning his relationship to photography. Man Ray is hardly ever pleased to have this aspect of his work emphasized, yet the subject must be dispensed with, for the sake of understanding what I call his clarity. His reputation as a photographer, which annoys him so much, comes from the fact that he himself knows more than any of us what photography really is. The fact that Man Ray extended the horizon of still and motion photography far into the future is for our purposes purely accidental. This is also the man who had the courage to write that photography is not art. He reminds us that the inventors of the camera were originally interested in competing with the artist of the day. Long ago, Man Ray discovered that art is not photography. For Man Ray there has never been a conflict between the two. Photography has always been an accessory for him, and an implementation to his painting. A camera, as he points out, has no imagination.

There is no more accident in pushing a button than in applying a brush stroke to a canvas.

Man Ray has always been, first and foremost, a serious painter. His quest for clarity was the driving force in his restless days as an art student. He was always changing schools and teachers, with his eyes open for anything to release him from the boredom of academicism. He had already acquired the technical equipment from his academic studies, plus an extensive training in architecture and draftsmanship.

But he was looking for something else. Therefore, he was ready to be excited by the Armory Show and the first trickles from across the Atlantic of Cubism and Futurism, forbidden entities until then.

After the intervention of the First World War, he became closely associated with such innovators as Duchamp, Picabia, Varèse and Stella who came to New York at that time. He describes his first meeting with Marcel Duchamp in 1915 on a tennis court in New Jersey, when Duchamp's entire English vocabulary consisted of the word "yes." Thus began a friendship and a mutual inspiration of great benefit to both of them, and most certainly to the art of our time.

During those days, they were working almost in a vacuum, indulging in a Dada of their own, independent of the European movement. Only a close circle appreciated or understood their activity. Sales or success were not even to be considered. At that time, Duchamp was beginning his break with Cubism. Picabia was veering toward the mechanical. Many of Man Ray's pictures from this period are on these walls.

In 1920, with the aid of Duchamp, Man Ray made his first voyage to Paris. Evidence of his immediate acceptance by the Dadaists is documented in the catalogue of this exhibition. For the next 20 years, he was part of Paris, doing photography, making films, exhibiting and participating in Dada and Surrealist manifestations, limiting his painting to no more than a dozen pictures a year.

The Second World War sent him back to America, and involved the tragic loss of many of his works. He settled in California, admittedly for climatic reasons, working again amid indifference, except for a very select audience. We also have here a generous selection of his work of this period.

In 1946, he married Julie, or Woman Ray, at the famous double wedding in Beverly Hills, with Max Ernst and Dorothea Tanning, later immortalized by a painting of Max Ernst. Julie is here tonight, and she is a true model for and to Man (Ray and Kind). By a wonderful coincidence, she is celebrating her birthday today.

In 1951, the nostalgia for Europe and for his old friends became strong enough to bring Man Ray back to Paris.

I insist that the essence of Ray's contribution is clarity. This, I think, will explain itself through the pictures in this exhibition. It is the clarity he sought and found during the early days in New York. A clarity he was able to contribute to the Dada and Surrealist movements. A clarity which helps to assure us that these great manifestations will never be dismissed as purely transitory.

Man Ray has never believed that there is anything purely spontaneous in art. The realization of a work can only be the result of thought and calculation, above all, organization. He will say that an idea cannot hold the viewer's attention more than the time it took to conceive it. Some of the things in this room might seem to belie this. The act of execution may seem to have been easier or more rapid in one instance than in another, but the work of art is made by the mind, not by the hand. A hurried thought can be hurriedly dismissed. A single brush stroke could conceivably take six months.

Like Duchamp, Man Ray is not overly concerned by finding a distinction between good and bad art. As long as art is creative, and not a reproductive process, the distinction hardly exists (art is not photography).

Like Duchamp again, I think you will agree with me after you have been with the paintings a bit, that there is little tendency on the part of Man Ray to repeat himself. He is not a joiner of clubs. Theme and variations there are, but there are many themes.

Unlike too many painters today, Man Ray has discarded none of the tools of his craft in order to exploit, let us say, matter. He believes in the full indulgence and use of all the elements. He has also respected humor as one of the happiest ingredients, and let us not be dismayed if some of these paintings seem to laugh at us, or cause us to laugh with them.

Yet, he is never blind to matter, and is as ready to appreciate the material aspects of painting itself (see the recent series of tactile paintings) as he is the poetic nature of the objets trouvés.

Much can be said about Man Ray, the inventor, but no more than you will see for yourselves tonight. Man Ray himself is not interested in what came first or who came first. We know the Rayograms justly bear his name.

Is Man Ray an abstract painter? He answered this when he labeled a series of paintings in a Beverly Hills exhibition as "non abstractions." He prefers to call some paintings non objectionable, rather than non objective.

Is he a Surrealist? He will answer this with the question, "Why?" He claims to see more Surrealism in daily life than on all the Surrealist canvases he has ever viewed.

Man Ray is all of these, and none of these. He is one of our most serious painters, and his interest is in clarity.

Serge Charchoune

First published in *Art News* 59 (March 1960); reprinted in
Charchoune (William and Noma Copley Foundation, 1963)

Cité Falguière, just off the Montparnasse end of Boulevard
Pasteur, is a tiny Impasse with a tradition of obscurity. It was
the home of Modigliani and Soutine, and it is there, living
almost as their ghost, that the painter Serge Charchoune is
living today.

I am not one to romanticize or recommend starvation and
obscurity for artists. Such notions are for bad novels. Yet there
is something so poetically proper about Charchoune's presence
in the Impasse that it is often commented upon.

Charchoune's obscurity is an obscurity almost of choice,
not that he enjoys discomfort or being so often passed over,
in spite of his recognition by so many of the intellectuals, but
because his modesty and, above all, the lack of aggressiveness
in his painting, marry so perfectly with the old place.

It is a great temptation for critics of his work to pass him
off as an intellectual's or a painter's painter. His most ardent
supporters include André Breton, Robert Lebel, Jacques Villon,
Max Ernst and Marcel Duchamp. Certainly painters do own a
great many of his paintings and painters have been responsible
for keeping his spirits up, but this is too easy a generalization.
Rather, his lack of recognition stems from his determined,
almost stubborn, refusal to paint aggressively in a period when
aggressiveness in painting is so much in style. I am happy to
say that the lack of recognition he has suffered is gradually
becoming a thing of the past and true to the quality of modesty

we are discussing, Charchoune shows no more surprise at his now more frequent successes than he did at the persistent indifference he endured for so long. He will tell you that he admires the violence of today's young painters. "But . . . I am a more complicated savage." He also admires the individuality of the Surrealists, perhaps his strongest defenders, but has steadfastly refused identification with the group, insisting that *métier* is more important than subject matter. Yet, is he really this far removed from Surrealist attitudes? "The abstract school," he has written, "includes the worst, but also the best. Art is the domain of ecstasy. The artist is closer to natural primitiveness. Nothing is created with premeditation. Instinct and subconsciousness, indecision and errors, are worth more in art than calculations and the knowledge of a banker."

In order to understand the obscurity from which he is beginning to emerge we must emphasize the gentleness of his painting, which tends to go unnoticed in a time when painting is often confused with gymnastics.

It helps to know him personally, and it is a delightful experience. He is over seventy now, quite thin, with an angular face and a mouth more used to vaguely smiling than laughing openly. His gray hair is nicely tinted by spots of color which come directly from whatever canvas he is working on, since his spectacles do not seem to sufficiently relieve his present shortsightedness. He will shock us occasionally by appearing in Montparnasse or Saint-Germain in a Sherlock Holmes deerstalker, and he has been known off and on to sport a beard. Patrick Waldberg tells me he once saw him with a moustache that entirely covered his mouth. He told him that he wore it to remind himself of the virtue of silence for, in his opinion, people talked too much. He dresses neatly, as though his clothes were not threadbare, and wears the dignity of a gentleman from an almost forgotten epoch. A friend is always greeted as *"chèr maître."* He is a born bachelor because he is a born recluse, almost a hermit. He is not incapable of flirting with a certain gallantry but this is part of good manners. His remaining passion seems to be a fervent love of country witnessed by his inability or unwillingness to give up his Russian identity or to believe that all will not be as it was once before. He moves in a world of exiled compatriots and there is a comic tragic tale of his formal visit to the Soviet embassy when, after dressing carefully for the occasion, he offered those of his paintings that survived him to his native village. He was surprised and hurt at how quickly he found himself in the street.

His tiny studio has an easel, one or two uncertain chairs and a shaky ladder to a shaky balcony where he sleeps. There is no room to back up to better view the large canvases he struggles to show you, and while he pants and wheezes, you must let him struggle for only he knows how they can be maneuvered. Even so, one is forced to witness near disasters. Meanwhile, they must be stacked against the only exit, which can be disconcerting to one given to claustrophobia.

Charchoune was born in Bougourouslan, Samara, Russia, in 1888, which a critic once remarked "doesn't happen to everybody." He describes his early years as lyrical, which I take to mean—and he admits it—that he was a lazy student. Being of Slavic back-ground, and given to dreaming by the banks of the Volga, so beautiful at Simbirsk, where he was sent because his town had no school of its own, this early infatuation had a most profound effect on his painting, and the lyrical flowing line, so suggestive of water or melody, is the constantly present entity in his canvases. It seems he painted against the wishes of his father, but managed to study painting for several months in Moscow, where he was able to acquaint himself with what was going on in Paris— Fauvism, Impressionism, Cubism.

Like so many of his generation, his arrival in Paris in 1912 was motivated by the need to avoid military service. There, he became involved immediately with Cubism, studying under Le Fauconnier, who had a great influence on him, as well as Metzinger and Segonzac. He first exhibited at the 1913 Indépendants.

Then followed two and a half years in Spain, where he worked primarily in Barcelona and some months in Mallorca. Here he had his first contact with Dada, which was to influence him briefly a little later, when he came in contact with Picabia's review, *391*, and the fabulous Arthur Cravan.

More important, I think, was the influence on him of the Moorish ornamental tiles, which appealed to his Slavic nature, reminding him perhaps of the decoration from the home he never stopped longing to see again. His first organized exhibition was painted in the style of ornamental Cubism.

Charchoune never winced at the criticism of being decorative, and if, for a while, his work was frankly decorative, he says it was because it fitted his Slavic background. He considers Kandinsky, though not as concerned with the actual matter of painting as he himself is, the father of modern painting, and along with his predecessor, Wroubel, feels that the contact with icons was finally established.

In a fit of zeal, inspired by the change of regime in Russia, he successfully volunteered for the Russian Expeditionary Corps in France. He did not consider himself an exceptional soldier, and he was happy to be discharged in 1920.

His brief courtship with the Dada movement came about through a chance meeting with Tzara while he was supporting himself as a book peddler in Paris. Some of his drawings and poems were reproduced in the *Dada Review*, but here again his retiring nature kept him from participating with the violent enthusiasm which characterized the group, preferring the company of his fellow Russians, exiled painters and poets.

While he denies participating in Dada as a painter, and had declined to participate in the Surrealist movement, it is interesting to note a series of paintings done in 1955 as the project for the illustration of Kafka's *Metamorphosis*. They depict the actual metamorphosis itself, with a sensitivity to the subconscious worthy of the most dedicated Surrealist.

After a trip to Berlin in 1922–23, where he went with the intention of returning to Russia, he suffered a political disillusionment which made final his break with Dada. Traces of the Dada experience remain in his work, and he was influenced by the mechanical aspect of Picabia's work. This, plus the fascination of the Moorish tiles he saw in Spain, his frank love of nature and the orthodoxy of his training, provided the raw material for his period of ornamental Cubism, and for a brief period of ornamental Impressionism.

It was at this time that he came in contact with Ozenfant, whose influence became less as time went by. As stated above, Charchoune does not mind being considered decorative, an anathema for most painters today, and it is perhaps the frankness with which he embraced the experiments that led him safely past the pitfalls. André Salmon, one of his earliest friends and defenders, describes him as a Cubist who surpasses Cubism, as the Seurat of Cubism: "A conscious colorist of the place given to volume by color." Marcel Sauvage compares his harmonies of tone to Juan Gris, and his sobriety of line to that of Braque: "Charchoune treated ornamental Cubism without giving in to abstract decoration." Charchoune considered himself a "lagging-behind Cubist."

This period of ornamental Cubism includes painting of still life and also many landscapes, treated certainly not representationally, but quite freely. There is almost always water, harking back to his childhood on the Volga—quays, boats, trees. He is known to have once remarked to a friend: "I can't live where I don't see water." Gradually, we see his obsession with music begin to dominate. We have seen it already in his Cubist renderings of the violin, a subject popular also with Braque, guitars of course with Picasso, and these artists, along with Klee, he has no hesitation in admitting as influences.

There were difficult years for him. He painted when he could. Often he had to seek employment to live, if only washing dishes. Occasionally, he received some enthusiastic recognition. His first contact with the commercial world was thanks to Salmon, who arranged his first important exhibition in 1926. He sold two-thirds of this exhibit at the Galerie Jeanne Bucher. He also had successful shows at the Galerie Auber, the Galerie Percier and the Galerie Bonaparte. But these were sporadic successes, the paintings appealing mostly to the intellectuals as opposed to the public, and left him worse off than ever.

Always a solitary man, personal experiences dominated more and more the subject matter of his painting. "I am responsive to all influences, those of the environment in which I live, that of the last little occurrence of everyday life, and of course, that of my colleagues. If I am moved by an exhibition, upon returning home, I usually begin to paint in the manner of the painter who impressed me." In referring to this statement, the critic Patrick Waldberg writes: "What artist is capable of speaking of his work with such lucidity, modesty and courage?"

To me he once said, "Whereas I paint today on the inspiration of musical experiences, I might, on seeing pretty girls by the Seine, start painting that experience." The concert is one of the great pleasures of the solitary man. Charchoune hears more music than he sees pretty girls by the Seine. Giulia Veronesi has said: "In a parallel between music and painting, Charchoune has found a source of harmony." I want to remind the reader of the accident involved. It could as easily be pretty girls by the Seine as the musical line which flows as pleasantly, for Charchoune, as the waters of the Volga and the Seine. Indeed, water and music are practically synonymous for Charchoune.

Charchoune has resisted Dada and Surrealism because of his conviction that he is an abstract painter. Yet, he freely considers himself an enemy of mathematics and science, and has never painted with any rigid theories. Edouard Roditi

makes the point that his musicalism is not based on any
theories of color and form. Rather, it is purely personal, as in
certain compositions of Klee, Kandinsky and Feininger, also
inspired by music. Nor must we forget that he wanders in and
out of the Louvre as often as in and out of concert halls. Still,
Charchoune considers himself stubbornly as an abstract
painter. Assuming we accept this, and assuming that there is
nothing in art more abstract than music, musical subjects are
attractive to him because of their convenience. His titles
are always "inspired by" this or that musical work. And he
has admitted to me that the works involved are merely a point
of departure. For me, they set the mood primarily through
color. Wagner with brasses is invariably splashed with yellows.
Boccherini is polychromatic. All this is abstract, if you like,
but there are occasionally undeniable subjects over and above
the flow of water or the musical line. These are so personal,
harking back probably to his years at home, as to be subconscious, and I am convinced he is not aware of them. In a somber
rendering of the Beethoven Funeral March, I found an image
so unforgettable and haunting that it has become part of my
dreams, a cross leaning precariously over what appears to be an
open grave. The subject is a funeral march and the image is
death. This concept, unconscious as it probably was, belongs to
the world of the subjective subconscious. In answer to the
question: "Are your works symbolic?" Charchoune made this
answer: "Not in the least. There is never a key. One should not
look for more than an evasion of reality, and an attempt at
transcribing a state of the spirit." Is he not bordering on the
Surreal in this attitude?

It is the contention of the most ardent admirers of Charchoune
that the monochromatic and, above all, his white monochromes,
are the most exciting of his later work. There seems to be an
attraction, somehow not destructive nor deathlike though the
temptation to see it so is there, a sort of photo-synthesis which

leads him to white. He has a habit (often considered disastrous) of reworking old paintings. White is a heavy color. I tried to lift one of his medium-sized monochromes, once a polychrome based on a Mozart theme and worked upon over several years, and nearly broke my back. All that time he had been adding white to it. If we admit, which I insist, that this is not a disastrous process, I may return to my premise that the enchanting characteristic of Charchoune is his modesty and non-aggressiveness. Let me muster some support. René de Saulier, *Nouvelle Revue Française*, February, 1959: "The works of Charchoune are the instruments of meditation, but plastic, which compare with Tobey and Arpad Szenez, as masters of white painting." Certainly, let us not forget Malovitch, Comte J. de Divonne: "Charchoune recognizes his hermeticism. He knows he cannot please the crowd. Some of us regret that he confines himself to sad tonalities—grays and browns."

This modesty, this desire not to offend by color, should not be confused with tastefulness, a problem which exists not at all for Charchoune because of the basic lack of sophistication in his personality.

Patrick Waldberg again: "One can pass a Charchoune painting without seeing it. In his light canvases the range of grays, creams, pinks or violets attains such a fine degree of subtlety, that the least lack of lighting risks letting them melt into the wall. The fact that a painter devotes his life to making almost invisible paintings seems astonishing enough to be worthy of note. The value of Charchoune lies neither in his nonexistent drawing, nor in the ascetic manner. It is the simple and naive juxtaposition of his strokes in a sort of discretion and modesty which confers on his best work their originality and charm."

Leon Degand: "His painting shines with no seductive extravagance, no exterior signs which attract one's attention. It even seems that he gets a sort of pleasure out of rendering himself half-invisible."

Considering Charchoune in the light of his self-definition and what observations we have been able to make, we have perhaps established him as an abstract painter whose charm abides in his modesty.

I cannot deny that Charchoune accepts this definition of himself; his behavior, as well as many conversations with him, bears this out. I can only suggest that here again his modesty is misleading. It is impossible for me to limit my enjoyment to the purely abstract aspect of Charchoune's painting.

François Hertel, of the French-Canadian Academy, has referred to Charchoune as a naïf of abstraction, an abstract painter in the sense that François Villon was a pure poet. The critic Charles Estienne has called him the last and most modest of the Surrealists: "His problem has always been to express himself without cheating." Lest the word *naïf* be misconstrued I must emphasize that this must not be applied to his technique which has a firm foundation and there is something wonderful in the sureness of his heavy impasto brushstrokes which invites one almost to want to eat his paintings. Perhaps the term best applies to his vision, his stubborn insistence on symmetry. One sees this aspect most clearly in his river scenes, perhaps the most personal of his paintings, where the water flows before perfect houses with perfectly placed trees. Waldberg calls these: "Homes for the soul."

His violin of 1948 is first a violin, then not a violin, analyzed almost out of existence before my eyes, only to emerge again more than a violin. A violin returning with its music! A poem of a violin! And invariably, I associate poetry with the Surreal.

The series of projected illustrations for Kafka's *Metamorphosis* is the closest approach to a Surrealist attitude toward painting that we can find in the work of Serge Charchoune. These are pictures of metamorphosis, descriptive of suspended intervals in states of being, inspired directly by the Kafka story. Also there is a curious portrait of Churchill, contemporary with the Kafka project, where the man and his cigar seem suspended in this same manner as though growing into each other. This pictorial metamorphosis, frankly descriptive, has much in common with his later monochromatic painting. The tendency of Charchoune to render his own forms unnoticeable, if not invisible, suggests a constant and perpetual metamorphosis, particularly appropriate to the rendering of a musical theme. Assuming that the paintings with musical titles are to be considered actual renderings of music, which I am convinced they are not, and Charchoune himself denies, then they would still be a step beyond, say, Mondrian's *Broadway Boogie Woogie*, in that the vibrations of tones are not achieved by bright contrasting color, but rendered poetically through a suppression of this obvious mechanical approach. The paintings which seem to start out with sharp tonal clashes, more often than not find themselves literally toned down through a series of afterthoughts. If then, he is not visually reproducing musical themes, but, as he claims, using such themes as a point of departure, is he not then personalizing the experience of viewing pretty girls near the Seine? Such personalization destroys any clear definition between purely abstract or poetically Surrealist art, if we think we need to use these terms. His closest friends hail from both camps.

It has proven too difficult to resist including the following document in the picture I am trying to give of Serge Charchoune. It serves as a mirror that he has held up to register his own image of himself and that of the world around him. I doubt if it will lead us to any conclusions about his paintings but should confuse and delight us simultaneously. The truths embodied in it are Charchounian and as such eccentric and charming. These are his convictions, the convictions that have produced the painting that we are considering here. In preparing this article I asked Charchoune for his views on what differentiated his later paintings from those he had done before. He either understood me badly, which is quite possible as French is not the mother tongue

of either of us, or simply wanted a declaration of his own
recorded, which is suggested by the fact that he wrote the
introductory paragraph for me:

*Now, with advancing age, and at the approach of the half century of his
Parisian life, Charchoune at my request, has thus determined the actual
state of the arts:
they are all ornamental,
their function is priestly.
It was Greek art which first, owing to its marble-like clarity, was the
innovator and which precipitated everything toward photography.
The affluence of the khans, shahs, rajahs, popes and other Napoleons
created the miniature; mechanics—Saintsulpician art, and finally,
democracy—the cinema. Now, painting is purifying itself in rediscover-
ing its predestined field of action. Actually, this impulse embodies
all humanity.
Gauguin, as a somnambulist (or animal-like or plant-like) owing to
his pursued surroundings wended his way toward the source.
His successor is Paul Klee.
The ascetic Cézanne, worshipper of El Greco, that ornamental
Impressionist who planted himself like a statue on the work of Poussin,
very consciously created constructive painting of Gothic, Romanesque
and Byzantine icons.
Mondrian (Cézannian) and Picabia (Gauguinnian) were both of
Armenian stock.
Gleizes and Picasso—of Spanish. The last has accomplished a titanic
task in bringing back art from the classical to the ornamental. He is an
African Raphaël.
Kandinsky and Chagall are Russian. The first of princely origin,
it appears, born in the depth of Asia, is an amalgam of elements: of
music, of mathematics, of icons and of Chinese ornamentalism. The
second: of hysterical Jewish music, of Orthodox icons and of Russian
"Images d'Epinal" (loubox).
F. Marc and other German Expressionists have struggled with the*

presentiment of the coming of ornamentalism.
J. Villon is a consolidator of Cézannism as well as the first step toward
the Saintsulpician ideal.
Arp is a perfect architectonic artist as well as Pevsner and Gabo.

These are personal views, as personal as his painting, almost naive
as his painting is almost naive: Charchoune is a man who lives and
works mostly in solitude, a solitude that does not have to exist
for painters today. It is something of a relief not to have to try
and place him properly in the contemporary scene. As the ghost
of Cité Falguière his uniqueness is assured.

Man Ray: The Dada of Us All

First published in *Portfolio*, no. 7 (Winter 1963); reprinted in
Man Ray: Inventor/Painter/Poet (New York Cultural Center, 1974)

In the summer of 1915 a rather Dadaistic tennis game was in
progress in front of a cottage in New Jersey. There was no court
delineated and no net. An American was shouting out scores,
"Fifteen love, thirty love." His opponent, or partner, a Frenchman
with an extremely limited vocabulary in English, replied to each
announcement with the single word "Yes."

These two men were the Dadaists of the Yes variety and
were destined to remain unique for demonstrating that affirma-
tive philosophy could be visually stated. But first, their mutual
enthusiasm and eventual collaboration was to comprise New
York Dada.

One of the earlier embarrassments the twentieth century
was to inflict on itself was the Dada phenomenon. It cropped up
by a sort of spontaneous generation in three widely separated
areas: in Zurich at Hugo Ball's Cabaret Voltaire with Richard
Huelsenbeck, Tristan Tzara, Marcel Janco, Hans Richter, Jean
Arp, and Sophie Taeuber; in Barcelona with Francis Picabia,
Serge Charchoune, and Arthur Cravan; and in New York at the
instigation of our tennis players. Intercommunication was to
come later. Robert Motherwell's admirable documentation
of the Dada movement dates the origins of Dada as a historical
movement from the beginning of the Zurich activity in 1915–16.
The book includes an account written by Gabrielle Buffet-Picabia
in 1949, in which she remarks: "A highly remarkable circumstance
which raises many questions is the existence in Zurich of a group

of painters and writers whose activities singularly resembled the New York group, although there was no possible contact which could have made known the one group to the other." She also records a meeting of Picabia and Duchamp as early as 1910, but one has only to reflect on the painting *Caoutchouc*, done by Picabia in Barcelona in 1909, to realize the independence of his research at that early date. She also remarks on Picabia's anarchistic state of mind when she first met him in 1908, and goes out of her way to compare the attitudes of Picabia and Duchamp at the time that Duchamp was working on *Sad Young Man in a Train*, a picture which is signed "1911." The Zurich group were valid revolutionaries already disgusted with the bourgeois motives that were producing World War I, and were determined to avoid participation in the debacle. The young Lenin was a frequent visitor at the Cabaret Voltaire. Dada for these people was negative in conception, and the participants merrily accepted Dada's inherent destiny to annihilate itself sooner or later.

Marcel Duchamp, the Frenchman of our tennis game, was to continue to say "yes" for the rest of his life, and so transcend the negative destiny of organized Dada. The American, Man Ray, was instinctively a Dadaist in the same positive sense. He was to import into France a humor he had absorbed from his native environment which he would eventually lend to the formation of Surrealism as the logical phoenix rising from the ashes of self-annihilated Dada. The damage wrought by these two stunning eccentrics on the smugness of drawing-room painting was catastrophic. It is no longer possible to think of being a painter without a thorough knowledge of their existence. The doors they opened can never be closed again.

Duchamp, not content with liberating form by a gigantic "explosion in a shingle factory," augmented the known dimensions of painting with his *Tu m'* mural, allowed the glass *Bride* and *Bachelors* to step out into actual unpainted space,[1] corralled the readymades to exist forever in our imaginations, and finally

1. *The Bride Stripped Bare By Her Bachelors, Even* (1915–1923), commonly known as the *Large Glass*.

essayed the acting out of art in personal behavior to the exclusion of all visible effort so often referred to as work.

In the case of Man Ray, myth will have it that he made photography into an art, a questionable accomplishment, as he himself is the first to insist. Myth, too, will sometimes have it that he merely reflected Duchamp, aided him in some of his experiments, and then dropped out of sight. Their collaboration in New York Dada and Katherine Dreier's Société Anonyme is recorded history. Reference to this collaboration on New York Dada can be found in George Hugnet's article *The Dada Spirit in Painting* and in Robert Motherwell's introduction to *The Dada Painters and Poets*. Katherine Dreier's acknowledgment of Man Ray as, along with herself and Duchamp, one of the three creators of the Société Anonyme can be found in her introduction to the catalogue of the "Collection of the Société Anonyme: Museum of Modern Art" for the Yale University Art Gallery. Their collaboration was natural, as that of two personalities similarly inspired with a mutual vision of possibilities of expression undreamed of until that time, and with the ability to incite each other to newer and bolder outrages.

And let us not forget that Man Ray was a painter before the famous tennis game, and had already succeeded in getting into considerable trouble all by himself. His own *Self Portrait by Man Ray* is characterized by a candor which he has gone out of his way to make as shocking as possible, establishing that truth can be much more delightful than *"son et lumière."* He had proved himself something less than a brilliant student in his Brooklyn high school, but had nevertheless won a scholarship in architecture of which he disdained to avail himself. As a high school graduate, he was on his own, and now would have to support himself by seeking employment. But he made the decision to be an artist.

From the beginning, his interest in art was merely a reflection of his interest in life itself. He tells us how he was motivated to enlist in his first life class by the chance it offered him of viewing an undraped human female, something he claims he had been unable to accomplish up to that time through purely social pursuits. This was all after hours, as he was already taking jobs doing lettering and layout—easy enough for him, as it involved the use of the same talents that had won him the unused scholarship. This natural flair for precision work stood him in good stead throughout his whole career. Once, he even apprenticed himself to an etcher of umbrella handles, quitting the job immediately because he was sure he had mastered the technique. His tongue was never more in his cheek than when he executed his first known work, a piece of pure Dada inspiration, the large *Composition* made in 1911 out of tailor's fabric samples sewn together.

One suspects that his interest in the human form remained consistently social. Already he was avidly aware of all that was modern in art and seeping into the New York galleries from the continent. While he was busily offending critics with his personal but rather Cubist renderings of nature (Man Ray called them "romantic expressionism"), he preferred painting his landscapes from memory (or better yet, invention), and was deciding to concentrate on the man-made in nature.

His first exhibition in 1915 was at the Daniel Gallery, in New York, and included paintings prophesying this style change, and one which prophesied war: a large, ominous Uccello-like canvas begun in July of 1914. The outbreak of hostilities occurred before its completion and the canvas was entitled simply *1914*. It can be seen in the Gallatin collection at the Philadelphia Museum. The influence of the Armory Show has been evoked in connection with this painting, but in retrospect the emergence of a purely personal style is more obvious. There is also the preposterous tiny landscape called *Man Ray 1914* which becomes ridiculously obvious only when the picture is hung upside down. It was in connection with this exhibition that Man Ray first tried

his hand at photography as a means of reproducing his own
work. He recognized immediately the subversive possibilities
of the camera.

After the closing of his apparently unsuccessful exhibition,
he was flabbergasted to learn that Arthur Jerome Eddy, a wealthy
collector from Chicago, had purchased six of the paintings at a
price that was going to make all sorts of things possible, including
a long desired move from Ridgefield, New Jersey, to New York
City. Eddy was then over seventy. He was a corporation lawyer,
an owner of race horses, had had his portrait painted by Whistler,
had brought the first Renoir into the United States, had been
a national fencing champion, and was reputed to have ridden the
first bicycle in Chicago. Elated by Eddy's encouragement, Man
Ray began work on a huge prophetic painting, to be concluded
in 1916, dealing with the subject of a rope dancer he had seen in
a vaudeville show and to be called *The Rope Dancer Accompanies
Herself with Her Shadows*. He intended to show motion by
transition between wildly contrasting spectrum colors. He had
been blocking-in his forms with cutout colored paper, but the
work seemed not to go well until by chance he noticed a disarray
of colored scraps, seeming like the dancer's shadows, beneath
the easel. I use the word "prophetic" because of the importance
that shadow was to assume as an added dimension to the *Tu m'*
mural and, of course, the *Large Glass* that Duchamp was to become
involved with later. The title too seems suggestive of the stately
The Bride Stripped Bare by Her Bachelors, Even. I insist strenuously
that there was no consciousness involved in these similarities,
hoping to suggest rather something inevitable. *The Rope Dancer*
was followed by a series of colored paper cutouts mounted under
glass and titled generally *Revolving Doors* which Man Ray refers
to as pseudo-scientific abstractions. They bear individual titles
such as *Orchestra, Concrete Mixer, Dragon Fly, The Meeting*, and *The
Legend* (based on an earlier large painting also called *The Legend*,
now in the Urvater collection in Brussels, and considered by

Man Ray as his first purely abstract venture). Man Ray says
that the idea of *Revolving Doors* may have been a subconscious
response to Duchamp's image of the *Chocolate Grinder*. He
remembers that there was a concrete mixer outside his window
at the time. The important thing is that they were both attuned
to making *Legend* from such images contemporaneously. Let
us not forget the titles worn by the bride's stable of bachelors
in Duchamp's painting.

His friendship with Duchamp was growing, as was his acceptance by the group which surrounded him and met frequently at
the home of Walter and Louise Arensberg. This included Francis
Picabia, Jean Crotti (Duchamp's brother-in-law), Albert Gleizes,
Henri-Pierre Roché, Jules Pascin, the composer Edgar Varèse,
the American painters Glackens and George Bellows, and the
eccentric Arthur Cravan. The idea for an Independents Exhibition
in 1917 was conceived at one such gathering, giving rise to the
twin scandal of the Richard Mutt porcelain (a Duchamp "ready-
made," merely a urinal, which was refused by the committee,
prompting Duchamp's retirement from all participation in the
exhibition), and the Arthur Cravan lecture, during which Cravan
was forcibly restrained from utterly disrobing before the lectern.
Man Ray exhibited his *Rope Dancer*.

Man Ray's second exhibition at the Daniel Gallery (works
executed during 1915–16) was scandalous in much the same
spirit. Exhibited were a handful of items or inventions to invite
the participation of the spectators: bells that would not ring,
a panel that would not hang straight. His third exhibition
(1916–17) included, besides the *Revolving Doors*, ten of the airbrush
paintings now considered among the most *recherché* of Man
Ray's works. They were encouraged certainly by the use of the
same materials employed in the job he was then holding—doing
lettering and layout for a commercial art firm; but also he was
intrigued by the idea of reducing artistic virtuosity to an absolute
minimum, and by the clean, untouched-by-human-hands look

of a photograph which it was a challenge for him to try to capture in paint. Duchamp was working away at his glass, a task which occupied him for nine years and was never meant for completion. At that particular point, he was scraping away silver mirror backing from the *Optical Witness*, a maddening job involving precision work with a razor blade. Man Ray was feeling superior in working at a technique that promised something almost instantaneous.

In the year 1920, through the enthusiastic patronage of Duchamp, Man Ray was accepted into the Katherine Dreier Société Anonyme, a name he quite innocently provided. Nominally he was the museum's vice president and on a more practicable level the house photographer. His original contributions were the spiral form of a discarded lampshade and an airbrush painting on glass with the ambiguous title of *Dancer* or *Danger*, the implication being that comedy and tragedy can dance on a single letter. The lampshade spiral succeeded in getting itself discarded a second time, according to its destiny, by the janitor, and Man Ray was forced to sculpture it out of metal to give it a protective pretension. It was bought by Katherine Dreier but has since again disappeared, although it has remained a motif in many of Man Ray's subsequent paintings.

Man Ray was becoming more and more intrigued by photography and was making some money from it through portraiture and the work he was doing for Katherine Dreier. He was able to record the aspect of one of Duchamp's optical machines an instant before it broke to smithereens, and was able to capture for all time the aspect of the *Large Glass* covered with six months' dust and resembling a lunar terrain. A memory of this remains in the glass itself as captured time. Intrigued by the phenomenon, Duchamp varnished and thus preserved this dust on a portion of the glass. Also, Man Ray and Duchamp worked together in 1920 on a third-dimensional motion picture project of Duchamp's. For developing the film, Duchamp devised a maze of nails mounted in the lid of a garbage can. The result of this was a complete disaster which Man Ray described as resembling seaweed.

They brought out a Dada magazine, *New York Dada*, together, through correspondence with the Dada group established in Paris. The cover was by Duchamp, the interior layout by Man Ray. It was a successful Dada venture in that there was just the single issue.

In 1920, Man Ray made the first of his personalized chess sets of unconventional form. Professional chess players could not have cared less. About the sets' interest is uniquely sculptural. Even Duchamp, who designed a set of his own probably about this same time, has always preferred playing with conventional sets, albeit he, as opposed to Man Ray, had attained a degree of skill where buttons might have sufficed for the pieces. To this day, Man Ray continues to design chess pieces. His silver and gold set of 1926, now in the collection of the Museum of Modern Art, is a triumph of simplicity based on geometric forms relieved by the single lyric concept of the knight, which was cast from the head of a violin. Contrary perhaps to popular conception, chess has not played a part in his life as it has in Duchamp's. He has never been an ambitious player, but he has been consistently fascinated with designing chess sets, of which there are many. Duchamp's designs were not executed.

Man Ray had begun to dream of Paris, more so now, as Duchamp had already left. An advance on a sale of paintings arranged by Stieglitz was to make it possible and, on Bastille Day, 1921, he was met by Duchamp in Le Havre.

In Paris, he was immediately ushered into the society of the reigning Dadaists: Jacques Rigaut, André Breton, and Paul Éluard, then met Gala, Louis Aragon, Dr. Théodore Fraenkel, attending physician to the poets, and Philippe Soupault. Francis Picabia was already at odds with the Dada group but Man Ray, who always was able tactfully to avoid the civil wars, struck up a friendship with him that remained in itself something of a Dada manifestation and lasted until Picabia's death intervened in 1953.

In 1921, Philippe Soupault, the poet and a member of the group publishing the Dada revue *Littérature*, decided to open a gallery, and what better Data gesture could there be than to launch it with a presentation of Man Ray, introduced to the French public as chairman of the chewing gum trust? Erik Satie was at the opening and was able to converse with him in English, and their friendship warmed at the corner groggery. As they returned to the gallery, a French hardware store was exciting enough to inspire the now notorious object, *Gift*, the flatiron studded with tacks.

Collaboration with Duchamp continued with the filming of the outrageous spiral puns of the *Cinéma Anémique* in the suburban home of Duchamp's brother, Jacques Villon.

Catherine Barometer, a colorful object seeming to be an instrument for measuring vaginal fever, and *The Board Walk*, a rather hard-edge abstraction destined to be shot many years later by a reactionary young manifestant, were exhibited at the Salon des Indépendants. But Dada had many years to wait before it became a commodity, and out of necessity Man Ray was becoming a professional photographer. There can be no question but that this was a real frustration, involving the necessity of making a living when he would have preferred to be painting. But because he was an artist and because he was a Dadaist, photography was to experience at his hands a revolution which it will catch up with only sometime in the distant future. Perhaps it was inherent in his personality to see all details of life somewhat out of context, or to be always expecting chance to provide him with opportunities for rich humor. In photography, accident was as much a part of his media as was his genius for observation.

Man Ray is resigned about his reputation as a great photographer. Quite simply, Man Ray was an artist who often, and during these years certainly by necessity, used a camera. There is no denying that he was able to put himself in tremendous sympathy with the device, thus establishing his triumph over it.

The same holds true with his motion films. By the most simple solutions, he managed to outstrip the imagination of an entire industry. In agreeing to make the *Mystery of the Château D.*[2] he accepted a weekend invitation from the Vicomte and Vicomtesse de Noailles (whose greatest achievement was getting themselves expelled from the Jockey Club because of their participation in the Luis Buñuel film *L'Âge d'Or*) with the understanding that he would bring along his movie camera. What he did do was to solve a proposition of Mallarmé's: "A throw of the dice can never do away with chance." It can almost be said that the film was made with a camera and a pair of dice insofar as Man Ray made sure that no fortuitous detail remained unexploited. Inspired to show a collision for a sequence in *Emak Bakia*, an earlier film, he instinctively set and threw his brand-new movie camera thirty feet in the air, the thrill and danger of the gesture becoming sealed into the film.

It was inevitable that he would "invent" the Rayograph, the simple result of allowing objects to be exposed to controlled light while spread out on photosensitive paper. There has been much useless discussion on who was first to stumble on this wonderfully ridiculous technique. That Man Ray was to work at this was a phenomenon that was inevitable: "A throw of the dice can never do away with chance."

Meanwhile, the Dada movement was running its course. As with human destiny, its death was spelled with its inception. Surrealism was emerging under the inspired dictatorship of André Breton.

It is important to note that Man Ray can be easily identified as a pure Surrealist as he can as a pure Dadaist. The three personalities that endured the transformation, Duchamp, Ernst, and Man Ray, had in common first a disinterestedness in the polemics and personality squabbles that mired and limited so many of the others; and second, a positive humor that transcended the purely negative expression of Dada which could but lead it onto political

2. *Les Mystères du château du Dé* (1929).

rocks. The most valid aspects of Surrealism are consistent with and an outgrowth of these positive aspects of Dada. Surrealism inherited the iconoclasm that was necessary for the break with tradition, and it was concerned with a creative humor which offered far more possibilities than the pure derision of negativistic Dada. For minds so equipped, the techniques of Surrealism—the Lautréamont equation of the sewing machine and the umbrella on a dissecting table, automatic writing, exquisite corpses, and so forth—all designed to free the imagination from its natural limitations, were merely a continuation of a research already begun.

The impetus of Surrealism is quite noticeable in the paintings of Man Ray of this period and actually seems to have restored his interest in painting, a medium he had all but set aside. His large painting *À l'heure de l'observatoire—les amoureux* (1932–34), inspired by a photographic enlargement of the mouth of Lee Miller, his favorite of all models, marks his return to painting. As the dates imply, he worked on it steadily over a period of years, while his involvement in photographic activity was at its height. This painting is one of the monumental conscious Surrealistic statements, satisfying the Surrealistic formula of distorted contexts, but having a warmth and a naive erotic implication that was embarrassing even to some of the Surrealists.

Because an artist has expressed himself in one way or another at a time preceding a more general preoccupation with such expression does not necessarily mean that he has influenced the world or that he has invented anything. But it does mean that he has been prophetic. I find such prophecy in much of the work of Man Ray. There is, for instance, the *Collage* of 1935, which was executed by merely fixing objects on a tabletop after his cleaning woman was through tidying up on a particular morning.

For Man Ray, the Second World War was a deep personal tragedy, a shock from which a side of him must never have recovered. He was there and he saw it coming. His mood during the days preceding his flight from Paris was elaborately noted

in an immense canvas bitterly entitled *Le beau temps*. He says
it was made up of eight separate nightmares from which he
had been suffering. Shortly after he completed it, the Germans
arrived, and he was there to see cruelties inflicted. When finally
he fled, with the occupation of Paris a reality and the armistice
declared, he left his property and most of his life's work behind.
He did not tarry in New York, where his Surrealist contemporaries were regrouping, and where his talents in photography
alone were sufficiently recognized to have made a comfortable
life possible. Instead, he continued, dazed by shock. The West
Coast was perhaps as far away as he could get, and there he
assumed the life of an exile. There is a noticeable change in the
spirit of his subsequent work, toward the more objective,
the contemplative, and the ironic.

It was during the California years that he executed a haunting
series of paintings based on mathematical objects once called
to his attention by Max Ernst in the Poincaré Institute in Paris.
They were handled in a way to poeticize their abstract austerity
with the footnote intention of poking gentle fun at his fellow
Surrealists in New York, who were allowing themselves to be
shown in exhibitions of abstract art. These pictures were titled
after Shakespearian plays and the series was called the
Shakespearian Equations.

Since his return to Paris in 1951, Man Ray has continued in
exile, or, as he prefers to say, is continuing "unnoticed." His
painting is even more contemplative, geared to the satisfaction
of purely personal problems, intended, as he says, to liberate
himself once and for all from "know-how." But lest one think that
he has lost his bite, I call attention to the devastating "Objects of
My Affection," with which he surrounds himself, such as the
untranslatable *Pain Peint*, a pun on several things.

The Russians, who have fostered a rather successful revolution
on themselves, prefer to have their own inventors of the airplane,
and have discovered a man called Popov (who also bears the

name of their favorite clown) who invented the wireless. Americans, who are conscious of having brought about a rather successful revolution in the arts, also tend to be niggardly in awarding credit in cases where it is due to Continentals or expatriots. It will be difficult to invent another Man Ray. In any event he prefers to be called "the American." His uniqueness is that mostly he used no hands. Duchamp and Man Ray are the only two I know who can wear this compliment. Man Ray has made his art from phenomenon, his collages from happenstance. Somehow, he has always instinctively found the shortest road from yesterday to today.

Marcel Duchamp 1887–1968

Originally published as "Marcel Duchamp 1887–1968,"
New York Times, Sunday, October 13, 1968

Because I knew him, I find it inconceivable to speak of Marcel
Duchamp as no longer living. For those who missed the
point of his greatest statement, he has not been among them
since he officially ceased painting years ago. Though he did
not die that long ago, he did define eternity, and he entered
immortality at the time he left the easel and took art with him
into creative life.

Had he been unwilling to share the experience, this would
have been a fulsome obituary—and this is not an obituary.

If Marcel Duchamp ever died, his phoenix Rrose Sélavy
(a name having endless possibilities of punning transformation)
mushroomed from the remains of a past he unshrouded when
he inked in a moustache on the Mona Lisa, creating for himself
and all of us a present in which the nouns "art" and "poetry"
are forged into a single word.

The word was lying around for a long while, and it should
not be suggested that he invented it. He was the first to discover
how to articulate it, and the word is *Yes*.

"... Art may be bad, good or indifferent, but whatever adjec-
tive is used, we must call it art, and bad art is still art in the same
way that a bad emotion is still an emotion."

Or: "There is no solution because there is no problem."
This was his way of saying "Yes" to the universe, the galaxies,
the magno-microcosms, the explosions, the implosions, nature.

★

I like to think that hearing him say this with his own lips once saved my life. This may be mere sentimentality but I gladly risk saying it. Isn't the universe too grandiose, or don't the movements of the stars lack time to hear us therapeutically? Can this vastness tolerate something as ridiculous as a solution?

Later it became "Yes" and "Chess" (fun and games with the laws of chance). Like Mallarmé he recognized the implications of a single throw of the dice. Like Lautréamont, he saw the beauty of mathematics. The *Large Glass* penetrates considerably beyond these implications to "canned chance" or "meta-irony."

Freedom, wherever it may lead, was the revelation of his phoenix. Marcel Duchamp was long since with the Milky Ways.

The New Piece

Originally published as "The New Piece," *Art in America* 57, no. 4
(July–August 1969)

My relationship to Marcel Duchamp was largely personal and
amicable. I do not consider myself an intellectual as a painter
and so never really got involved in the intellectual analyses of the
Large Glass or the notes that accompanied it. Duchamp's influence
on me as a painter was enormous but strictly poetic, having to
do with what I assumed to be my understanding of his humor
and his philosophy as expressed through his personality.

I would like these few words to be considered as sheer speculation or as nonsense. Otherwise it would not be fun to write and
probably no fun to read.

I insist that I understand why he perpetuated the myth that
he long ago stopped working. I will oversimplify this here. It must
have seemed to him the most direct way to ensure himself the
privacy he needed to continue working in the light of what was
already becoming an exaggerated reputation, because, "Yes,
Virginia," there is a final monumental work which occupied him
for approximately the last twenty years of his life.

Only a detail of the exterior is reproduced here; the interior
will not be photographed. To begin with, the work must be
viewed through two peepholes like eyes in a Halloween mask.
No other method of viewing it should be considered—no
walking around it or touching it, or admiring it sculpturally. The
piece is to be merely experienced. Marcel Duchamp was always
an ardent supporter of happenings and had what was to me
a prodigious patience in lending his time to them. This piece is

in many ways a happening, but a short glimpse of it makes its effect for a lifetime.

The *Large Glass*, too, because of the materials chosen and the specially invented perspectives, was intended to convey an experience other than merely looking at a picture. There can be little doubt that Marcel intended this new piece to be an extension of the unfinished *Large Glass*.

The title of the *New Piece* is as enigmatic as that of the *Large Glass*:

Étant donnés: 1. la chute d'eau
2. le gaz d'éclairage
MD 1966

It is equally as "frank" in the sense that it is a monument to certain actions between men and women that some editors still delete if called by a certain four-letter word. But we are willing to use a four-letter word, *life*, and wink slyly.

The Bride and the machinery that makes her female are represented carefully and symbolically in the *Large Glass*. In the *New Piece* she and her moving parts are represented with disarming frankness. In the *Large Glass* her partner in *life* is represented in multiple by the Bachelors, the complex of all men. In the *New Piece* she is holding her man in a gesture that is (again) disarmingly frank, but what she is holding is the lamp of illuminating gas. The illuminating gas was represented in the *Large Glass* as emanating from her.

The illuminating gas and the waterfall (or the "falling of water" as the reading in French allows) are the basic elements of the activity between men and women that the two pieces are concerned with ("Eau et gaz à tous les étages"). The falling of water achieving the symbolic splash in the *Large Glass* is represented in the *New Piece* by what appears to be an actual waterfall contrived by Duchamp with a Rube Goldberg–like machine disturbing a painted postcard landscape, thus achieving, as in the *Large Glass*, the symbolic aspect of the falling of the water. The isolation of the all-important symbols—falling water and illuminating gas—remains a constant in the two great pieces.

Another speculation I am drawn to make concerns the game of perspective that Duchamp plays with himself in the two works. Richard Hamilton has explored with final expertise the aspects of perspective in the *Large Glass*. These seem to function totally in reverse in the *New Piece*. The nude ceases to exist where vision cannot reach, channeled as it is through an oval hole in an inner brick wall. I will not comment on the significance of this as I have not fathomed it beyond the obvious. Nor have I fathomed the faggots upon which the nude is reclining; here the obvious seems too dangerous, and perhaps one does not have to look at all. But I know these branches were collected lovingly by Duchamp in expeditions to the country.

I might speculate, however, on the two different kinds of precision involved (precision being typical of Marcel and time never being of the essence). The tense precision of the *Large Glass* is replaced by a more relaxed precision in the *New Piece*. The nude herself in the *New Piece* recalls his painstaking work on the *Glass*. He built her skeleton, he stretched her flesh, he bought her wig. The similarity stops there.

The door through which one peeps was cut down from familiar doors in Cadaques, Spain, where Duchamp summered for so long. The bricks that surround the door were filched from building sites. The intricate waterfall is housed in a cookie tin. The whole thing is set on a checkered linoleum mat-room for further speculation, I guess, for chess buffs.

But I cannot intellectualize on this piece of Marcel's; I can only feel it. I have experienced it. I can close my eyes and see it in detail anytime I choose. Both pieces I'm sure were motivated by Marcel's need to be busy—or, better perhaps to say quietly, his positive feelings about life. The materials for both pieces came from daily experience, endless and random. The work was an enjoyment of patience; the difference between the two techniques might represent the difference between spring and fall—which may finally explain the autumn branches on which the nude reclines. The work was signed "MD 1966." Does this mean that the *Large Glass* was finally finished? I do not think so, but I do think its implication was restated with finality.

Portrait of the Artist as a Young Dealer

Text written c. 1974; first published in French translation as "Portrait
de l'artiste en jeune marchand de tableaux," in *Paris–New York*
(Centre Georges Pompidou, 1977)

The first thing I did when I got out of the Army was to marry. She
had a colorful brother-in-law, John Ployardt, who was an artist. I'd
never met one before and this impressed me.

In those days I drank perhaps more than I do now. So did the
brother-in-law, John Ployardt. He had a job doing Mickey Mouse
and such for Walt Disney. He hated Disney and called himself
a Surrealist.

I didn't know anything about such things. I'd been trying to
be a liberal, which consisted mostly in passing out handbills for
poorly attended meetings. I'd played tennis with Henry Wallace
who beat me badly, lobbing in a fat old way. I had a hangover. He
was a lousy winner and criticized my lifestyle.

The brother-in-law, John Ployardt, shared my kind of lifestyle. He taught me about Surrealism and encouraged me to
think exaggeration.

I needed this. Surrealism made everything understandable: my
genteel family, the war, and why I attended the Yale Prom without
my shoes. It looked like something I might succeed at. As I understood it, there were two aspects of reality: the public or social one
that we are taught where everything has a name, the reality we
must communicate with; and the private reality that is the reality
to us alone, which needs poetry and above all metaphor to communicate. This is the super-realism. And it made sense.

Southern California in 1946 was a most unlikely and certainly
a most unnecessary place to proselytize Surrealism. As Man Ray

once said, there was more Surrealism rampant in Hollywood than all the Surrealists could invent in a lifetime. The natives didn't know this. The place was an intellectual desert, never mind the film industry's pretensions to the contrary.

There was a mausoleum of a structure way downtown called the Los Angeles County Museum, which harbored some misacquisitions of William Randolph Hearst and a few stuffed animals. It was to become the first of many institutions to refuse the Walter Arensberg collection. There was a converted Chinese movie house in Pasadena which inherited paintings from time to time. There was Vincent Price. At that time he had had something to do with a museum of contemporary art that failed. He had better luck with Sears Roebuck.

It was an enormous community. There was wealth and few collections. There were many antique shops, damned few galleries.

Old Earl Stendahl was a candymaker turned art dealer. He operated out of his sumptuous old-fashioned California residence on Foothill Blvd, residential Hollywood. He dealt profitably in pre-Columbian art, most of which he sold to his next-door neighbor, Walter Arensberg. Arensberg's great collection was intact and could be seen by a polite telephone call. But Arensberg had become passionately concerned with proving that Bacon wrote Shakespeare.

Stendahl also dealt in Tamayo, Siqueiros, and Rivera. Occasionally in Impressionists too. He let Sam Kootz show off his Picassos whenever he came to town. They were relatively cheap but seemed expensive at the time. I bought one once as an extravagance and hung it in my bedroom at home. It caused a couple of my family's friends to walk out of the house in a rage. It sent Henry Wallace and his entourage into gales of uncontrollable laughter. I was pissed off, having lent him my bedroom and slept in a so-called gameroom in the cellar. Anyway, he wasn't elected. My friends wouldn't believe it was not a reproduction. My maid liked it. When I decided to become a Surrealist,

I gave it to the County Museum. They put it in their cellar. Stendahl had a sweet Rousseau, quite small, which I didn't buy for $2,000.

Stendahl was charming. He told wonderful stories which he didn't expect to be believed. He never pretended to be more than a merchant and thought all artists were mad. He champagned the Man Rays and the Ernsts after they had doubly married in Beverly Hills.

The consciousness of the dealers in the area had not progressed beyond the Mexicans or the post-Impressionists. Dazil Hatfield had a plush gallery in the Ambassador Hotel where there had been a famous Coconut Grove which famously burned down, sort of the El Morocco of the West Coast. Hatfield survived and stayed conservative. He also exhibited the paintings of Mrs. Edward G. Robinson.

Jolly Frank Perls didn't push his luck too far either, but handled some good Paul Klees.

There were a few very well-meaning pioneers who sincerely tried to push the local artist just discovering abstract art. They were mostly dreadful painters, except maybe Lorsa Fiedleson and his wife who weren't dreadful and worked hard. But they were dreadfully abstract.

No one in their right mind would have considered trying to open a Surrealist gallery in the California environment, which, of course, is what we decided to do late one whiskied evening. In the white haze of the morning after, we were both too proud to perish the thought.

The brother-in-law, John Ployardt, quit his job with Disney, which his wife and family depended on. I sold my house. For a gallery we rented a bungalow building on Canon Drive in the heart of Beverly Hills. The rent itself should have curled our hair. We bought ourselves a bronze plaque which read "Copley Galleries." I remember it cost two hundred and fifty bucks.

We were convinced we would startle the community by our very far-outness and that Surrealism would be a new household word for the idle rich. We scoffed at the suggestion that there might be anything to learn about going into business.

Françoise Stravinsky, Igor's daughter-in-law, was to be our secretary. She was sweet and it was a great arrangement. She didn't type too well, but we kept this from her. We'd send her on errands and I'd type the letters over. I didn't type too well either. But we adored her and it was a great name to bandy about.

The maestro himself used to come to the openings at the gallery and was as much an exhibit as the paintings were. He usually wore a cape and looked a bit like Dracula.

Once he had us for dinner. He was an exuberant host and very much a poppa in his home. Being Stravinsky in those days didn't pay all that much and the family lived together rather modestly. Vera, his wife, had been with a gallery. There was a small personal collection. Soulima, his son, was working at being a concert pianist and played Chopin and Scarlatti for us in a warm and Russian way.

Stravinsky was a Scotch whiskey drinker. For cocktails he staggered in with a huge, heavy heirloom of a silver tray with at least two dozen bottles of different brands of Scotch. He asked us what we wanted to drink. As we were leaving he patted us all on the heads and admonished us to "Be happy." I was moved.

Being the dedicated Surrealists that we were, we were sharply aware of the necessity to demonstrate that popular and primitive art were by nature surreal. André Breton and Tristan Tzara had established this and had both assembled collections to underline the point. Before that there hadn't been much collecting of these things outside of museums. Picasso's *Les Demoiselles d'Avignon* was a revolutionary painting in that he incorporated primitive African art formally into his imagery and the imagery of modern painting.

There was also contemporary primitive art. We thought to steal a march on the art world by looting Mexico a little. I like to maintain that the reason Mexico has produced no important painting is that it is Mexico. The light of Mexico annihilates all but the most gaudy colors. The Mexican Indians always understood this. The academies didn't.

Mexican popular art is sold in every market place. It cost literally nothing, is impermanent, and generally loud in color. It is made by peasants with materials such as clay, rattan, wood, paper, or papier-mâché, with colors they manufacture out of the ground. The subjects are functional in that they are usually religious or superstitious. They are full of fantasy, the awareness of death, and the Indian cruelty that the Church allows to pass as zeal.

We headed for Mexico in a jeep station wagon and, after drinking up Mexico City, headed further south to Pueblo and Oaxaca, stopping wherever there was a market. We filled the jeep in no time at all and thought to arrange to have the rest shipped, which was sheer folly. These arrived long after there was the gallery, and the US Customs, sure that no one would ship such junk unless they were smuggling something, tore everything apart searching for dope. It was a hell of a trip though.

Prior to all of this, I'd been drinking in San Diego with an ex-marine who'd been psychoed out of the Corps during the war, which should have told me something. I remember he had a beautiful redheaded wife with green eyes and a couple of kids. He had a tale about going over the hill in New Guinea and becoming an honorary citizen of a native village. It was right out of Joseph Conrad. He described in detail art treasures he picked his teeth with every day. And of course he'd made a map.

I shared this tale with the brother-in-law, John Ployardt, and Ralph Altman, a lovely man, a dealer in antiques (because he had to) and primitive art, and an anthropologist in his own right. We bought our ex-marine a ticket to New Guinea and equipped him for safari. We got a telegram from him every time his boat docked along the way. It was always for bail money. We finally got discouraged and left him rotting somewhere, I suppose, since we never heard from him again. Altman was nice about it though.

Man Ray was vintage Surrealist, the only one such living in the Los Angeles area. We needed him badly.

We found him in a courtyard of studios across the street from the "Hollywood Ranch Market," open twenty-four hours a day. It was a pocket of Europe incongruously located on Vine Street a few blocks down from the infamous Hollywood and Vine intersection, which tourists think is Hollywood, and where small-town girls run away to, hoping to be seduced by movie producers. His wonderfully dated Cord sedan was parked on the street eternally unticketed.

Man Ray was in semi-hibernation practicing what he termed his "masterful inactivity" or "being continued unnoticed."

We aroused him one morning just before noon and were told through the door to come back at a more decent hour. Later, after he had shaved and dressed, he seemed grudgingly glad to see us. I think he was touched by our youth and lunacy and our homage. He was suspicious though, until he realized the extent of our lunacy and the abjectness of our homage. He let us in.

There was a large rectangular studio room. The light of the perpetual California sunshine came in pearly through a wall of windows which he had never allowed anyone to wash. He said it gave him a diffuse light he preferred. We assumed it reminded him of the grey of Paris. Everything was shabby-tidy and crowded. Much seemed made, invented, or just discovered by him, oddities pertaining to him acquired maybe through years of wanderings in second-hand shops. An impressive collection of only his own painting jostled for available wall space. A lot had to do with chess—sets and boards of his own design were on tables everywhere or affixed magically to the walls. His "objects" were everywhere too, some hanging from a balcony.

His wife, the lovely quiet Juliette, slim and boylike with close-cropped hair that Man himself attended to, was herself part of the feel of the place. It was immediately obvious how she worshipped him, very much a one-Man woman, if I can get away with the outrage.

We were initially uncomfortable in our awe while we stammered and blundered to the point of our visit. It didn't seem that it was going to be easy.

I didn't know then of the ritual we were having to go through. It was necessary that he impress us that he was a tough bird to deal with and he growled at us a bit. That was Man Ray. He could never play this role convincingly for very long and his awareness of this deficiency depressed him. We put our tails between our legs and waited. The aggression subsided and he seemed glad to have it over with. Our proposal must have kindled something in him, an exhibition of his choice, with ten percent of sales guaranteed.

He'd had a respectable exhibition a few years before in that Pasadena place. The local art critic who undoubtedly doubled on obituaries had ridiculed him scurrilously with a text of double talk. What reputation he had was as a photographer. This infuriated him, prompting his convincing article or essay, "Photography Is Not Art."

He had too few friends of the kind he needed. There was Allie Lewin, the producer at MGM, a tiny white-headed aging imp, along in years and quite deaf, but with a sense of humor one could live on. He was always turning his hearing aid off at the slightest threat of boredom. He loved Man and his work and the Surrealists. Those of them who knew him, loved him back. He included their paintings in his films whenever he could get away with it. He commissioned an Albright brother to do the picture of Dorian Gray. He'd run a competition for *The Temptation of St. Anthony* to be used in the film *Bel Ami*. Max Ernst beat out Dalí. He used Man's portrait of Ava Gardner along with a casual shot of one of his chess sets in the film *Pandora and the Flying Dutchman*.

Earl Stendahl of course was his friend, as was Paul Cantor who had a brave gallery then but had to finally become fashionable, and Paul Wescher who was a refined man acting as curator for the private collection of J. Paul Getty. Otherwise it was slim pickings for kindred souls. Maybe I couldn't have met him at a better time. Anyway, we've been friends forever.

Man Ray had been one of the last of the vulnerable to escape from Paris. As far as he knew at the time, it cost him his mistress, beautiful Black Adi, his Citroën, his country house, and his studio with paintings and negatives representing years of work. After the liberation, he did recuperate most of the latter through the dedication of the Maison Lefebvre-Foinet, which I'll have to talk about later.

In New York he discovered and ran off with his Juliette. They headed West, hitchhiking part of the way with a necktie salesman.

He had every reason in the world to expect that Hollywood would be interested in him. His reputation as a photographer had preceded him and the intellectual elite were aware of his avant-garde films, *L'Étoile de mer* and *Emak Bakia*. What he didn't know was that "avant-garde" were dirty words in Hollywood. They wined and dined and flattered him and listened to his excitingly outrageous ideas with carefully deaf ears. They had no intention of letting him near a camera.

After the nervous social preliminaries described, he accepted to show with us and the condition of ten percent guaranteed purchase. If I'd known then what I know now, I was a crook. He reflected his gratitude by providing us with an introduction to Marcel Duchamp.

We now had a stable of one. The brother-in-law, John Ployardt, and I headed for New York to pick up more Surrealists.

I'd been born in that town but didn't remember it. I'd played there on college weekends. I'd manned anti-aircraft guns there, in the middle of Central Park during the first winter weeks of the

war. Kids used to throw peanuts at us on Sundays. I'd crawl out
of my pup tent and sleep at the Plaza whenever I got a leave. I'd
known Times Square and Coney Island.

But neither of us knew the New York we were out to conquer.
We arrived with a list of the worst possible restaurants, provided
us by Californians.

We stayed at a fleabag hotel in Gramercy Park recommended
as Bohemian. The next morning the manager called us in and
accused us unnecessarily of having girls in our room. We were
almost terrified enough to head home. We were hayseeds. We
were being thrown out of galleries.

It was time to play our only trump card, our reference
from Man Ray to Marcel Duchamp. It could be done only one
way but Man Ray had given us our instructions. It was all very
Arabian Nights. First you sent a telegram to an address over
a beauty parlor on 14th Street. If you got a penny postcard back
(there used to be such things), your wish had come true. Our
Chinese cookie said to meet him in the lobby of the Biltmore
Hotel at noon the next day.

The Biltmore Hotel, we found out, had more lobbies than
buttermilk has flies. An hour and a half later, we found what had
to be Marcel smoking a pipe in the recesses of a couch built for
a lot of people. Only he could be Duchamp, a little shabby but
dignified, like maybe he was waiting for a bus. He appeared
amused by our groveling apologies. "But not at all. I like it here.
I often come just to ride the elevators." Somehow we could
imagine him doing just that.

We took him to a rather dreadful place for lunch, Luchow's.
I remember the head waiter had to lend him a tie. Even so,
we got put in a corner. There was a painting of a very sinking
ship in an awful storm, old and probably Dutch, frowning down
at us. Wanting to impress him or just to find something to talk
about, I remarked what a silly piece of shit I thought it was. He
spent most of the meal pointing out to me what was good about

it. But it wasn't mean, the tongue was in the cheek, it was easy, we felt we'd gone to high school with him.

He took us to the studio above the beauty parlor on Fourteenth Street. It was an empty and anonymous room. I seem to remember an incongruous bathtub in the middle of the bare floor. Nothing on the half-plastered walls but a hank of clothesline hanging from a rusty nail. There was a chess table set up with clocks to time moves, along with a lot of loose tobacco and burnt matches. There was one chair and one orange crate in case there'd be a game. There was, I suppose, a bed somewhere.

Anyway, we memorized every word he said to us in his relaxed and easy way, attaching mystery and profundity, going over it late into the night. Finally we had met the Grand Sorcerer.

For the rest of my life I called Marcel Duchamp my best friend. This is not meant to imply I was his. There became a need though for me to see him periodically, a few times a year maybe, I called it recharging my batteries. "There is no solution because there is no problem." "Yes and chess." Yes because there was no need for no, there was always chess. He was Aladdin's lamp and for us he was "Open Sesame."

Marcel sent us to Alexander Iolas. This was sensible. There were businessmen he could have sent us to, some of them we'd already struck out with. We had sort of a three-and-two count with Sidney Janis. (He later sent a letter of encouragement to us which I'm sorry I didn't have framed. It was warm and touching but of course he did see how addled we were at the time.) I got to know Julien Levy much later, and we are dear friends now. He doesn't even remember throwing us downstairs and I still tease him about it. There were other possibilities, Kurt Valentin, Pierre Matisse, who later did work with us generously. We stayed away from Peggy Guggenheim out of loyalty to Max Ernst. This could have been a mistake but it wasn't. Many years later I found myself liking her. But she had been pioneering with another plough.

Marcel rightfully assumed we were mad in the sense that Iolas was. He also certainly understood that the passion Iolas had for his artists, Ernst, Magritte, Brauner, Bérard, et al., didn't have too much to do with successful industry and commerce. He made us a good match.

Iolas had the Hugo Gallery. There was a Madame Hugo. I always wondered who she was. The gallery wasn't much. It was on the second floor of a brownstone, I remember. It had blue velvet walls. Iolas was a reformed ballet dancer, with a fantasy totally his own which involved attempting to support his artists whom he was as broke as. His loyalty was fanatic. We about fell into each other's arms when we approached him with our identical fanaticism. We were in business together before it occurred to him to wonder who we were. I don't suppose I ever found out who he was, or better what he was, except that he was Greek, raised in Egypt which maybe makes him Coptic which wouldn't matter anyway, except that perhaps it might explain the background of his morality. No one we had to deal with in the whole experience of the gallery treated us more fairly. He shared all expenses and disappointments with us without complaint and others were less generous. But obviously Anglo-Saxon ethics did bore him. Back then his English was bad enough to be sheer poetry and I so regret not having kept his Krazy Kat letters. He dearly expected us to bargain with him. The presents we got were recompense for whenever he felt he'd bettered us.

But not to get ahead of myself, because I am tempted to write much more about him here, his flights of sheer wisdom amid totally destructive clowning were an important part of our education. He did give us much of the material we needed for our California gallery. He also became the wildest friend we were to have.

One day when we were in his gallery, a gaunt cadaverous Charles Adams–like character wandered in with a heavy paper shopping bag. He didn't expect to be noticed and we assumed he belonged there. But we were mesmerized when he rather ritually disemboweled his package. One after another, he arrayed a floor full of magical toylike boxes, each one quite a wonder. They were like rooms or windows or stage sets. Palaces for owls, equipment for blowing bubbles against skies of world or astrological maps, burlesque lines of celluloid lobsters, homes for owls, colored sands just to be shaken. His name was Joseph Cornell. We bought all his boxes and took him to lunch. He looked hungry. Afterwards he asked if he could have an ice cream soda. He seemed afraid we would say no. He talked of California as though he'd heard about it. He'd had an uncle once who'd gotten as far west as Chicago. The uncle was a traveling commercial man who'd dealt in rugs, successfully too. The nephew didn't seem to feel he was of the same stuff.

It was funny talking to Cornell. We had to leave our world and enter his. We were never sure we'd find our way back.

The boxes astounded us. We would of course have a show of them. He asked no more than a hundred dollars for any one of them. This worried us. They were treasures, conceived of nostalgia and fantasy; nostalgia for childhood, old times and places and beautiful people long dead. Something like what Chicago meant to him.

Roberto Matta Echaurren was the one-man electric company of the forties in New York. Since René Crevel's death, he had inherited the junior chair of the formal Surrealist hierarchy, only to say he had the youth and it seemed the genius to go with it. He was Chilean, in his thirties, was sinfully handsome and wore brocaded shirts. He was working apparently not too successfully on the second of what would be a lot of marriages. His painting promised everything. He talked wildly, too, with a sort of conversational Midas touch. He could make something gold and wonderful of the most trivial and banal. Duchamp had sent us

to him, and he was certainly our cup of tea. He worked, as he
spoke, with dazzling energy, sustained by a well-digested understanding of Duchamp and the beginning of what was to be an
astoundingly important collaboration with Gorky.

We dined at the Mattas with Maria Martinez, married to a
Brazilian ambassador, very much of a sculptress, perhaps once
beloved by Duchamp. She was all energy too. They were discussing a project and there was hysteria in the air. There would be
a single sheet magazine called *Instead* which would make comic
strips forever unnecessary. *View* magazine was about dead. It was
the only intelligent New York reflection of the vitality of the
Surrealist presence and was going to be terribly missed. *Instead*
was to be exactly what it called itself, "Instead" of. It fared like
so many beautiful ideas, dying after four issues.

We did have a brief, unsatisfactory lunch session with Isamu
Noguchi whom we somewhat admired and were interested in
showing. He was unpleasant and wanted to know, since we made
a point of labeling ourselves a Surrealist gallery, what guarantee
would he have that we wouldn't show a sculpture of his next
to an old shoe. Since we didn't like his question, we didn't offer
the guarantee. That one ended badly.

This is what New York proved to be for us: Duchamp became
part of our lives and our philosophies forever; we'd come under
the discombobulating spell of Joseph Cornell from Utopia
Parkway, Flushing, mad Iolas with his blue velvet walls, and
Instead of Matta. There were nights too in the Village with a few
of our own wild kind, among them Bernard Pfriem and Pete
Petrov, who did understand what was happening. They were
both promising painters. Petrov was an extraordinary draftsman
who somehow failed to persist.

In hindsight it was a hell of a time to be in the East. The
Surrealists had been in residence in New York as refugees. Nothing
would ever be the same again.

Americans don't like being beholden to Europe. But American painting was coming into existence. It's simpler to understand if we see Surrealism as what it was meant to be rather than a movement which it never was here. What it was always meant to be in terms of painting (more so perhaps than even Breton realized) was an opening of doors to the poetic possible through which contemporary art was going to penetrate. We have suffered a lot of confusion by denying this source, but maybe this had to be or how else could an eager generation rid itself of its artistic inferiority complex. Surrealism is still a dirty word here and America is supposed to have invented modern art by itself without having to be beholden anywhere. Along with Galileo's eyes and Van Gogh's ear, there were Mona Lisa's mustache and the Matta–Gorky tragedy. All this is gratuitous as I was only invited to write about the Copley Galleries in Beverly Hills.

Back on the Coast we felt very veni, vidi, vici. The first thing the brother-in-law did was to buy a monkey. The only explanation I ever got from him was that there was prestige in being possibly the only gallery in the world with a monkey. The sense of this escaped me, and I might have been more tolerant if the monkey hadn't been such a son of a bitch. The brother-in-law explained that it was a capuchin monkey which had significance with commedia dell'arte. I had to assume this had something to do with Surrealism.

There was one more Olympus to climb and we wanted to tackle it while the momentum was still with us. Next to Duchamp's the most exciting name we knew was Max Ernst, the one greatest painter of all, greater by far we thought than Dalí, who even then we were sure was being corrupted, greater for us than Picasso whom we saw as merely an old master.

Marcel had wired Max that we were coming. We drove five hundred miles nonstop across California, through a desert cold night, through dawn mirages to Max Ernst land, the Oak Creek

Canyon of Arizona, a landscape that Max had painted before he ever saw it. We felt vaguely familiar there ourselves through our knowledge of his paintings. Max had forewarned himself of this destination many years before.

Here our luck just missed falling flat on its face. Duchamp's telegram got badly garbled at the Sedona Country Store, which was the only faucet from the outside world. He had been expecting Duchamp himself. It showed on his face as we climbed out of the car. Worse still, Dorothea had returned from the hospital that morning after a serious operation. It was no time for us to be there and a long way back the way we'd come. Again we were groveling apologies and were astonished to be invited in with what almost seemed like enthusiasm.

Like Man Ray, Max Ernst was in his own way another exile hermit. Being a German in France, he had been in a situation where both sides in the war could only decide to want to incarcerate him, and he had been a prisoner in France. He was in retreat too from a marriage that had not suited him and had been scolded by the lady in her book and by the press, which accused him according to Max of moral turpentine. All he really did was to show preference for and fly away with the beautiful Dorothea Tanning, as American as apple pie and very much a painter in her own right. Max was also rather proud that all this put him in the dog house with André Breton.

In spite of its beauty, the Oak Creek Canyon and the settlement of Sedona (which was all it was then) was not particularly lively. This worked in our favor. There were few people he could communicate with there. The nearest old friend was Man Ray as far away as Los Angeles. The last time they'd been together they'd gotten civilly and doubly married in Beverly Hills. All described it as pretty much of a lark.

Otherwise, Max was cut off from his peers, under something of a cloud. His paintings weren't moving and his only neighbors were cowboys.

We'd sought them out out of admiration, and they were flattered and they were hospitable under difficult circumstances. The friendship still lasts.

We stayed several days, eating, drinking, talking. Dorothea was a magician. She made fantasy meals in the kitchen and we never knew she'd been out of the living room where the boozing was going on. Mostly we vied with each other to make the most outlandish jokes. Max always won, but he had two other languages to work puns on. Max was Loplop, king of the birds. It was his court and we were his jesters. There was no trouble about a show.

The Copley Galleries was ready to open its doors. We were sure we'd be successful. What we had to offer was the next best thing to the San Francisco earthquake. We were full of ourselves, heedless of any advice or caution.

The day we opened, the monkey bit the brother-in-law. Our first show was Magritte; paintings, gouaches, drawings, all thanks to Iolas. The opening announcement was a honey—a white page chopped out with Magritte's symbols, bird, leaf, key, pipe, to show a black underpage. The catalogue had sepia renditions of Magritte drawings. There were over thirty paintings, some of the great ones.

We had had free drinks which attracted a mob we thought had come to see the pictures. Some had. We were our best customers at the bar. After a while, we turned the monkey loose. He was scared and didn't like it. He leapt on pictures and unwelcome shoulders. It was a wild night and we figured we had half the town there. We were going to be talked about, if we didn't sell pictures.

The next morning we had hangovers and the gallery needed cleaning up. No one came by. The monkey was getting badly on our nerves. We needed some activity to reassure us. It happened as we were about to close.

A wealthy Californian lurched into the gallery. Not only was
he a mogul but he was a known collector. He was extremely drunk
but he knew what he was about and he knew about Magritte. He
wanted a drink and he didn't like to drink alone.

At home our separate wives were putting separate roasts
into the oven. Our initial client was lecturing loudly and learnedly
on Magritte, periodically waving his empty glass demandingly
at us.

At home our wives were taking separate roasts out of the oven.

Our client was now onto dirty stories. He had a repertoire.
Meanwhile he was having us set up Magrittes on the easel that
all good galleries have in the back room. Also he was calling for one
more round. At home separate roasts were getting cold. But we
knew that if we all stayed on our feet we were in the process of
our first sale. That part of it was touch and go. At home separate
tempers were rising.

Just before all was lost our client determined on an oil and
a gouache, perhaps the best of each we had, scrawled clumsily
across the face of a check and headed for the door as though
he might throw up. We couldn't read anything on the check but
decided to submit it as legal tender. We found our way home to
cold roasts and cold wives who weren't in the least impressed
that we'd had a successful first day of business.

We never saw or heard from the mogul again but the check
cleared. When we closed the gallery six months later we sent
the pictures by messenger to his address. In the next six months
of the gallery, we sold another picture. This time we never
got paid.

The great thing about having a gallery is living in rooms with pictures. Pictures go through the skin by osmosis. Eyes have nothing to
do with it. Magritte is a perfect case in point. His paintings taught
me this. They exist for other reasons than being seen. His images
have happened. The toes have become the shoes, the breasts have

broken through the nightgown, the leaves have become birds, we are never surprised by Magritte's surprises.

I did not meet Magritte until a few years later. The impression I had from his letters was that he was pleased by our concern with him, and that as an artist he was concerned with pleasing. All was matter of fact.

It was even more disconcerting on meeting him to have the impression italicized that he didn't have the personality of an artist as I had known such animals to be. He could just as well have been a pretzel salesman. He was stout, grey, jolly, prosperous looking. He was a Brussels bourgeois down to the shine of his suit. He was identical to his neighbor as his house was identical to his neighborhood. Once, in response to improving fortune, he bought a larger house. I went to the new address and couldn't tell the difference.

His home was furnished with the characterlessness of what was sensibly adequate, available, inexpensive, and contemporary; no fantasy. His own paintings, even the most outrageous ones, seemed no more out of place than the antimacassars on the sofas and chairs.

It is quite true that he painted in his dining room. He showed me where he kept his paints in a drawer where housewives usually keep napkin rings. No spot or stain gave him away.

I painted with him once across a chess table in my home. We were painting bottles, "I'll give you mine if you'll give me yours," sort of thing. He worked with the efficiency of a dentist, holding the brush at the end between thumb and forefinger like a gourmet eating Brussels sprouts. He frankly and modestly considered himself the greatest painter alive, as though how he painted established the fact. What he painted didn't seem outlandish at all to him.

His wife, Georgette, apparently a long time his model, blended perfectly. She was neither beautiful nor fashionable, only extremely pleasant and occasionally embarrassed when René waxed gross. She seemed to adore him in an uncomplicated way.

And there was always the God-damned dog. Like his houses, his dogs were always the same. He just kept outliving them, nasty rotten spoiled miniature Spitzes, sharp-nosed and yappy. He'd switch from a white to a black one once in a while. I like dogs but these ones always hated me and I suppose everybody. Magritte played this for what it was worth. The dog was always an excuse for not going where he didn't want to go.

He liked his beer and wine but no hard stuff. Also he liked to make off to the chess club with the boys. It was as much for the beer as for chess. He would play a dozen or so bleary-eyed opponents on a dozen or so boards, winning most of the time and preening like a peacock. He had me fooled for a while, till I realized it wasn't that much of a chess club.

He was a great one for dirty stories and there is nothing in the world like Belgian dirty stories. They are based mostly on scatology rather than sex and it takes a strong stomach to survive the sessions, which usually occur after a meal. I have seen banquets end up that way with cultured dignitaries trying to get each other to regurgitate really splendid dinners. He liked his vulgarity vulgar. He liked to laugh with his belly. He liked to shock Georgette, who in turn seemed to like being shocked.

We had an affinity for each other and he said I was the only one he would visit with away or overnight. He used his dog mostly to keep this from happening.

My wife at the time came to me on one such occasion when he was our guest, quite enraged and demanding I turn him out. He'd been pinching her tits. "But you don't understand," I said, "he's Magritte."

The Belgian government wanted to do a film on him. He insisted the scenario be his own. It included a sequence of Georgette eating a banana which he ran backwards.

I had a friend in New York, an executive with an office several floors below ground. He thought I could get Magritte to paint him a window. Magritte proposed to do a window looking out on a brick wall.

Magritte used to keep a notebook of his imagery, loose drawings in spiral binders. He was quite willing to give one of these up to another friend of mine who liked to order his Magrittes like breakfast. It finally amounted to about forty gouaches. "Now one with a sleigh bell and a sinking ship, etc." Magritte saw nothing unusual about this.

It has always amazed me that Magritte's paintings pose no problems for the uninitiated. The man on the street can accept him immediately, maybe sooner than the sophisticated collector or museum person. The answer of course must be that Magritte was much more of a man on the street than a sophisticate. He asks so little of us, nothing really intellectual, just that we enjoy his metaphors.

The brother-in-law and I had a crumby attitude toward local artists. We were dedicated to Surrealism. One day a couple came to us. They were both artists and they painted together. He from the left, she from the right. When they met in the middle, they told us, all sorts of wonderful things happened. We threw them out. This bothered me ever since. We should have looked at it.

The Cornell show was something we had to believe in. It took courage to do it at that time, and we thought it was our courage that would win for us. We were ourselves infatuated with the pieces. They were dream toys, nostalgia from all our childhoods. They were made with a cabinetmaker's integrity. We'd bought them and they were still embarrassingly inexpensive, so much so that we had to double the prices just to live with ourselves. We priced them one hundred to two hundred dollars and added a percentage for Cornell. There were about fifty items.

We worked on a combination announcement-catalogue trying to keep ourselves in the mood of Cornell. All was to be royal blue and white. The lettering was randomly torn out from romantic typographies, like a ransom note. The catalogue looked like it had been done on a sewing machine of a typewriter. As an afterthought, we all but papered the walls and ceiling with these flyers. We rented a white high-wheel bicycle and draped it with blue velvet. We presented the boxes themselves on shelves in alcoves where bookshelves had existed in the gallery rooms. The result was quite beautiful and publicly disastrous as it proved forbidding and claustrophobic to anyone not already drunk on Cornell and we were the only such two in town.

Again, there was a crowded cocktail opening. Initial response was encouraging and we thought for a while checkbooks might start flapping. We spent the next month alone with the boxes. We ended up giving them away to good homes as one would with puppies. The brother-in-law's wife made lamps out of hers.

Cornell blamed us for the fiasco claiming we loused it up by doubling the prices. He was sulky with us for a long time. One never knew where one stood with Cornell. With him you were always better off dead. Better still, female and dead. Or in a pinch, female, alive, but unattainable. He monumentalized the ballerina Alicia Markova and he loved Lillian Gish from the movies he remembered. In the case of Markova, he had a treasure of memorabilia, old programs of performances, old tulle that might have hemmed her skirt. These things would show up in boxes dedicated to her memory. In the case of his movie loves, he was somehow able to collect miles of film footage which he spliced together with implications known only to him.

The boxes were poems, literal and surreal in the purest sense, though to what extent inspired by the Breton bunch is not known. While he was in America André Breton constructed about half a dozen rather similar boxes, but reflecting very much his own poetry. I don't know who inspired who.

Cornell lived quite celibately with a spastic brother and an ailing mother, address Utopia Parkway, Flushing, New York. It is probably correctly rumored that the boxes were originally toys to amuse his bedridden brother. They were then the beginnings of an extraordinary expression of a fantasy world.

The boxes consisted of such things as astrological soap bubble sets with pipes and dreams included. There were quivering rabbit shooting galleries, celluloid red lobster quadrilles, whole drugstores in little bottles, deserted chateaux with forests growing out of their windows. There were sealed books with windows to view passing words. There was a paperweight of paper. There were sandboxes of colored sands, deserted hotel rooms in far-off Paris.

Cornell was an extreme recluse. It was a voyage for him to leave his house. He did his loving from afar, protected from reciprocation.

His letters were collage, like valentines, on colored papers, with paper lace or sachet or pressed flowers. That was when he wasn't pouting. One never knew when he might open contact again.

It was a strange, lonely month in the gallery with these lovely, unloved toys, with a public staying carefully away and no children passing through.

There was no question but that the monkey wasn't happy with art, which must have been why he hated us so intensely. He was queer for garage mechanics. The proprietor of the gas station across the street used to invite him home to dinner. He would sit at the family table with a napkin under his chin, a knife and fork in his fists, and smile for the children. These people actually wanted the monkey.

We had misgivings when we uncrated the Matta show. I wish I could see these paintings again. Matta doesn't seem to know or

care what happened to them. Years later he said the last he'd
heard of them, they'd been confiscated for one reason or other
by Italian customs officers in Rome. Apparently he never made
a serious effort to reclaim them.

They seemed too much like abstractions for our catholic taste.
In retrospect, I would say they were among the best paintings
he ever did, painted just before the boom was lowered on him
at probably the high point of his career. Two great influences
had been working on him. First there was the meta-mathematics
of the Duchamp *Large Glass, The Bride Stripped Bare by Her
Bachelors, Even*. But Matta's imagery was visceral, almost bloody
as a step beyond Duchamp. He had been best known till then
by what has since been tagged as his "jewel paintings." These are
still considered his most digestible work. They had great intensity
of transparent color and literally shone like jewels. They also
had a nervousness, very much a part of his personality, and a
violence such as found in what Wifredo Lam was doing at
that time.

Secondly these new paintings were done at the time of
his close association with Gorky, an association which was just
on the safe side of collaboration. The two men had almost
been thinking alike. Matta was more full of beans than he would
ever be again in spite of his continuing reputation of being
irrepressible. The Gorky tragedy was waiting in the wings, and
I don't think he ever survived it. A friend recently quoted Matta
as saying, "I wasn't in love with his wife, I was in love with
Gorky," on the surface a typical Matta quip, and probably quite
full of truth. This does not suggest homosexuality but merely
positive affinity, damned important to twentieth-century
art history.

More than a few of the paintings were loosely composed, with
reminiscences of the Duchamp *Glass* with a personal imagery
comparable perhaps to Gorky's, but still this side of abstract art
or what would soon become known as Action Painting. There

were two large mural-size paintings which reflected his appreciation and assimilation of Diego Rivera's contribution to mural space, the incorporation of platforms to magnify what could be stuffed into this kind of space, something Matta has always freely admitted. The paintings explained themselves to us during the month that we daily lived with them.

It was another startling show for us, another very wet and crowded opening.

That it did result in my knowing Matta was something not to be sneezed at.

The next time I saw Matta was in Paris when much had changed for both of us. He had been drummed out of the café court of Breton for moral turpentine. I was divorced from wife and gallery. We had both lost fifty pounds. We passed with no recognition on the way to meeting each other.

I saw him again in Italy. Then he was married to a third wife who was a film starlet. She had very tiny ears and knitted a tie for me. They'd made a son that he named Pappagano.

Like his painting, Matta's conversation was enormous gesture. He worried about and never succeeded in becoming able to paint small pictures. I told him the answer was to get small brushes.

We shared humor, humor of ridiculous situation, sometimes involving others but mostly ourselves.

He was a great marrier and baby maker. Politically he was the aristocrat of the left wing. He espoused sheer communism whenever it reared its inviting head, but never let this get in the way of his living. He was as welcome in salons as he was in meeting halls. He avoided riots. He could always get his audience to entertain ideas that had never occurred to them before. He could get society folk to join hands around the dinner table because he was pushing love at the time.

When his wife Malitte was pregnant, she had a tendency to miscarry and a five-flight walk up to their apartment behind

the back of Diderot's statue in Saint-Germain-des-Prés was not
recommended. I was able to kidnap them to my country house.
Matta and I both worked during the day and kicked around what
we'd done at drink and dinner time. It was fun. I once got him
to promise to teach me perspective. He came to my studio and
was about to start the lesson with a piece of charcoal poised
professorially. He then threw down and stamped on the charcoal
and said, "Are you trying to get me to ruin you?"

The baby began arriving one morning at an outrageous
hour. There was a great deal of running around and phoning the
American Hospital. Only months later did we realize that we'd
all been stark naked during most of the excitement.

Matta is always trading paintings for houses all over Europe
and for suits and Italian pointed shoes. He supports his many
children. I'm always amazed how he manages this. Since he's
always painting, I guess it figures.

He amazes me too in his ability to put his paintbrush down
on any pretext. There is no such thing as interrupting him.
He likes talk and people as much as his privacy to work. This
I envy.

It was at the end of the Matta show that the monkey decided
he'd had it with us. All I saw was his streak as he headed down
Canon Drive and across Wilshire Boulevard against a red light,
causing near accident and people to swear off drinking. There
was a movie house right there and he disappeared from view
underneath the turnstile. The phone in the gallery was ringing.
It was my wife who'd just cracked up the Studebaker. I called
the gas station across the street and asked the boss if he really
wanted the monkey. He said yes and I gave him the monkey
and went to recuperate my wife.

The monkey stayed in the theatre during the run of *The Babe
Ruth Story*, sometimes making scandal by hopping onto ladies'
shoulders. When the movie changed to *The Rope*, he left and was

finally cornered in the ladies room of the Security First National Bank next door.

Living with the Tanguy show was exquisite. The vast night-like landscapes, peopled with boneyard presences casting mile-long shadows, somehow failed to terrify. They constantly metamorphosed, nothing was static or seemed the same twice. They anesthetized and one had to dream with them.

The pattern was the same: grand opening, lots of booze and some celebrities, suspicions of success, teasing interest in specific paintings, even one sale that was never paid for.

The entire press consisted of one man who liked to drink. He'd do away with a half bottle of our best bourbon, go home, and feeling hostile, write his review. I rather liked him. He knew enough to understand he was being paid not to like modern art, but he couldn't really leave it alone. The paintings attracted him almost as much as the bourbon.

I didn't get to meet Tanguy until a year after the gallery closed. I met him through René Lefebvre. I'm not sure just how I met René Lefebvre or how he got to be my best friend. He was the kind of a friend you assumed you always knew. His family had always existed too.

The Maison Lefebvre-Foinet had been manufacturing fine art colors forever; canvas, brushes, et cetera. I once visited the ranch where the trees were grown from which twigs were burned to make charcoal sticks, and I'm not kidding.

The shop existed at the intersection of the rue Brea and the rue Vavin in the heart of Montparnasse, the Sixième. These were sleepy streets during the day and a raucous area of nightclubs and carefree prostitutes when it got dark. I knew that it was an old establishment because a huge tree had been growing a long time through the roof. They'd hidden Man Ray's car from the Germans under the floor of the garage.

The mother of the family was legendary simply because she had outlived the father who had been legendary before. The family policy was to provide colors for artists who seemed to know how to paint and couldn't afford it. The story goes that Douanier Rousseau used to drop off small painted canvases chez les Foinets as an attempt at recompense. The mother would wash the paint away to salvage dust rags. I do remember her with a ton of keys around her waist going from room to room locking behind her and unlocking ahead. René tells of a family christening gathering when he substituted goat turds for the traditional chocolate candies that always went with this kind of event.

I guess René was in California on business. One morning someone left a packet of colors on my doorstep. It was my first continental compliment.

After the gallery demise, I met René in New York. He wanted to introduce me to Tanguy. We drove up into Connecticut together. First we stopped off at Roxbury to see Sandy Calder. This was great because Calder was a delightful bear and let me see his studio. Seeing his studio was astronomy. He opened a barn door on an infinity of moving parts, a barnful of mobiles. Opening the door gave breath to the life inside. I remember there was a gong which was always almost ringing; most of the time it didn't happen and the drumstick and gong would start the pas de deux again on separate orbits to almost ring next time around. It was like the last act of *Tristan and Isolde*, or a good lay.

We refreshed ourselves at Calder's and when he heard we were going to Woodbury to see Tanguy he wanted to come. A cloud crossed his wife's countenance. Calder asked us if we could first stop in at a cocktail party he'd committed himself to.

There was no room for a man his size in the car we had. So we had to follow his vintage topless touring car. It was strange seeing a bear drive it. It was hard to keep up with him.

The cocktail party was a mob scene in somebody's small apartment somewhere. It was a problem not to spill my drink on myself.

Later, we did get to Tanguy's by following Calder again in his roller-coaster gondola.

Tanguy lit up when we arrived with Calder. His wife didn't. She'd been working to keep Yves temperate. Calder's presence harbingered defeat. The men embraced each other like two people who knew how to drink together.

I really didn't get to know Tanguy that day, except through what I saw of his house and his studio. The friends had much to talk about and the wife was tense and intimidating.

It was a nice old farmhouse painted pale yellow, otherwise typical of what one hoped to see in that part of New England. It was on a knoll and I think there was a pond nearby because I seem to remember some ducks.

I remember the billiard table in the living room because I didn't expect it. There were also ice cream parlor tables and ice cream parlor chairs with backs that looked like the script of old legal documents.

The studio was a whitewashed horse's box stall in a barn. The wife, Kay Sage, had one identical and next to it.

Yves's stall (being a male chauvinist, I didn't look at hers too closely) was something I've never seen outside of a hospital. A solid old French easel was equipped with a bar of spiraled wire on top to hold a mall stick for close work. His tubes of paint were filed or pigeonholed underneath the easel in trays of cubbyholes. Also there were surgical-looking tables.

Artists work differently. Some are slobs, some are tidy. Yves's studio was as tidy as his painting.

Since the departure, arrest, and probation of the monkey, there was a happy vacuum in the animal aspect of the gallery. Except the brother-in-law couldn't leave well enough alone. He probably

would have been a zookeeper if he hadn't decided to be a Surrealist.
The next thing we had on our hands was a bird. It came to us
through the children of Beverly Hills, who do exist there in spite
of massive birth control. This particular crew were in the bird
business. They'd found the secret that made it all clear sailing. A
bird that bites will never bite again if properly busted on the nose
in the first place. These kids would buy up incorrigible birds from
pet shops, tweek them in the beaks whenever they got aggressive,
and had them tamed in no time. They had them all lined up
on the handlebars of their bicycles peddling them as tame birds,
which they now were. The brother-in-law couldn't resist the
opportunity to buy one. The bird was sweet and tame and
bird shit was easier to deal with than monkey shit. What we got
was a cockatiel, a nice guy with a crest and colored exactly like
Tanguy's palette, dominantly grey but with orange and red and
lots of yellow burstings. He would come when we called, follow
us around or eat at our ears, and I finally got to love him though
we never cured him of shitting on paintings. I forget what we
called him. Or maybe her.

The Man Ray show had been a long time aborning. We saw a lot
of Man. He was the only one of our artists who was constantly
available for the planning of his show. This had its disadvantages
too, from a dealer's point of view. Artists, like mothers-in-law, are
often better appreciated when a certain geographical distance is
maintained. Not that we didn't love Man Ray, but it was going to
be perforce less of an interpretive effort on our parts, much more
his own show. In defense of dealers, the mounting of exhibitions
is a creative thing, without which nobody would be able to enjoy
the business. Also I don't believe artists hang their own shows
as well as a neutral can. They are too close to their own creative
agony. They tend to favor their later work at the expense of the
earlier. Maybe it's a way of fighting off old age. New work always
needs time to get loved.

We didn't know till the last day whether or not Man was going to let us have the photographs. He resented his reputation as a photographer. Some people didn't know he had ever painted. He had written and constantly preached that "Photography is not art." By this he meant that his photography was merely another activity that he as an artist indulged in. He liked to say that it didn't matter which end of the brush the hair was on. In the end we got our way by promising him carte blanche and it turned out about the way we'd hoped it would anyway.

Besides an announcement and a catalogue which exploited a photo self-portrait of Man with only the left side of a beard, we published an unbound folio of essays and reproductions, which included a photograph he'd done of a nude through a lens where a spider had made a home and a web. The shadow of the spider fell strategically and the web emanated from that strategic point. The book per Man's instructions was called *To Be Continued Unnoticed*. It included the essay "Photography Is Not Art," and the aforementioned review he'd gotten on his Pasadena show. Revenge sometimes comes late. We also published a bound book of twenty-six drawings, *Alphabet for Adults*. It mattered not too much that we couldn't sell these publications, since we found out later we were trying to sell them for less than they cost.

The show was a complete retrospective of paintings going back to 1914, objects such as the metronome which swung an eye and the flat iron with carpet tacks which destroyed as it pressed. The "object" was peculiarly a Surrealist invention which was originally considered little more than a game. All the Surrealists indulged in object making and it is unfortunate that not enough of them remain.

There were a lot of photographs and rayograms, the latter a process of his own invention, images accomplished in the darkroom without a camera with things composed and exposed directly on photographic paper. Man Ray stands out as a pioneer in photography primarily because of his disrespect for the camera, his discovery of the wonders of the darkroom. Once in the making of his film, *The Mystery of the Chateau D'—*, he risked a valuable camera by throwing it high in the air and happily catching it. The result was a giddy spiraling vertiginous experience. Photography was perfectly suited to the exploration and exploitation of the accident, an activity Man Ray may have acquired through close collaboration with Duchamp.

Cubism had had its effect on Man Ray—though, as to be expected, he expressed it with tongue in cheek. He personalized it with mannequin-like figures with tubular appendages. The mechanical wooden mannequin one buys in art stores already realizes this and he often used them directly in his paintings. He couldn't resist putting them in sexual positions and had done an unpublished collection of photographs of them which turned out to be more erotic than if he had used live models. Apart from the making of objects, he liked incorporating them in his painting, often altering them to make visual puns which he emphasized with titles in either English or French.

There was a series of more recent paintings, the *Shakespearean Equations*, based on the concretized mathematical equations found in a remote and dusty Paris science museum. He painted the forms faithfully but in obscure contexts and colors, titling them after the plays of Shakespeare.

Man Ray was one of the first to use airbrush in painting and there was a series of poster-size images he'd done with airbrush on cardboard, *Revolving Doors*. There was an Arp-like nude torso in which the white paint he'd used oxidized to a beautiful marble-like texture. I can't remember if he wanted me to believe that he had calculated for this.

We also had the famous lips called *Observatory Time, the Lovers*, dated 1932–34. They were the lips of his favorite model, Lee Miller, done from a photograph, floating now over a dark impressionistic landscape of blue and grey with the breastlike demispheres of the observatory in Los Angeles's Griffith Park. Since they're practically life size, the two lips can seem to be embracing human forms if you want them to be. We were chided considerably for this phornography.

Chess was important to Man Ray, as I mentioned, a passion he undoubtedly inherited from Duchamp, though he was never the player Marcel was. This had to do with their divergent personalities. Duchamp was made of patience. Man Ray wanted to cut all corners to everything. Chess was a subject in many of his paintings and we exhibited a number of the sets he designed. I have never figured out why the Surrealists developed their fixation on chess. I could have understood it if they hadn't gone that extra step of actually playing the game. I find it strictly sado-masochistic. Of course I went through the motions myself, and finally surrendered to the suspicion that it is a wearying, time-consuming pastime that undermines the ego. I suffer weeks after a defeat, my tail between my legs and all self-confidence gone. It is, I suppose, the infinities of possibilities that develop during the course of a game that leads chess players on. Only Duchamp developed into anything of a strong player and I once had to watch him be annihilated because a well-meaning hostess embarrassed him and a chess historian into playing a match. The historian offered his queen about as soon as he could shake her loose. Duchamp, and even I, knew the roof had fallen in.

I usually play almost respectably until my mind wanders to sex or something, and then I lose my queen by oversight and the preceding hours go down the drain.

The only one I ever knew who dared take a move back was Tristan Tzara. He was better in the won/lost column.

Chess masters are like dachshunds. They tend to be mad, have paralysis in the legs, and don't live long.

Surrealists have always liked to design sets. Tanguy fashioned a stunning and most playable set out of a broomstick handle, cut at different lengths and angles and painted in his own grey colors with a board to go with it.

Max Ernst sculptured a wooden set and every piece was very much a Max Ernst.

The Man Ray sets were equally Man Ray. Already his silver set was in the Museum of Modern Art. It was based on Cézanne's reduction of form to cubes, cones, and cylinders. The king was a pyramid, the queen a cone (French pun involved here), the bishops sort of bottle pots to go along with a French–English pun (*fou* equals crackpot). The castles were cubes, the pawns were spheres. Only the knights made no sense. They were cast fiddle heads, quite beautiful. Everybody knows the knight's move makes no sense. The great thing about playing with the silver set is that it makes one a cautious player. No one likes to lose pieces of silver.

According to Man Ray serious chess players are notoriously indifferent to unconventional pieces, claiming they can play with buttons. They don't allow their imaginations to go too far beyond chess and they never see the pieces they are playing with. But designing chess sets can be a medium in itself. Curiously it seems only Surrealists have succeeded at it. Man Ray designed many sets. He designed the first magnetic set to be played in bed. One wonders how many marriages have been ruined that way.

Man Ray has always been an inventor of ideas. He invented a portrait of the Marquis de Sade, since no real one has ever existed. It is now invariably used as the frontispiece for books on Sade. His work is rarely lyrical though when it is, it is apt to be poignant. More often it borders on the harsh, the almost disagreeable. His work must be read as well as seen. The relationship of an underlying idea to the visually apparent has to be mined for. The full impact is always delayed. He is only now being appreciated. No way in Beverly Hills in 1948.

The gallery had a patio on the street which we'd never use for anything, though it would have been great for sculpture if we'd ever needed it. This we turned into a sidewalk café for his opening.

Man made us a sign which read "Café Man Ray." In place of the traditional awning, we hung up his coat-hanger object, a progression of geometrically doubling coat hangers hung from holes in each other's extremities and making a floating pyramid oscillating above rented round tables. We rented red checkered tablecloths too but couldn't do better than the regular folding funeral chairs. We served red wine and French bread and got our wives and Françoise to make up gallons of onion soup. Some people had the trots the next day but we never found out whose soup it was.

Again the big turnout, the big party. There were a smattering of Hollywood personalities. Our favorite was a character actor we all know who always personified the English butler. He drank which he never did in the movies, where he just held trays of booze. He had two bodyguards, probably there to protect the studio's investment and keep him from drowning in the onion soup. He sounded just as he did in his films. "Madame, if you cannot refrain from this kind of drivel, you will commence to bore me," all in authentic, very British accent.

It snowed in Beverly Hills the day we opened the Max Ernst exhibition. It had never snowed before in Beverly Hills. It never has since. I am sure it never will again.

We had a bright idea for the announcement. There was an unusual photographer-painter who lived near Max in Prescott, Arizona. His name was Frederick Sommer and he had a slightly unhealthy fixation on the imagery of decay. He photographed garbage heaps, decomposing rabbits in the desert, the backside of an aging woman through the window of a rotting frame house. (In this case, I think it was his wife and his house.) He once gave me an artificial leg as a present. He really wanted to be a painter. His painting consisted in preparation for painting. He stretched and prepared canvases of various sizes and hung them on hooks and screw eyes from the beams of rooms and rooms, all ready to be painted. They never were. What paintings I saw of his, for there were really almost none, were dull monochromatic abstractions having nothing to do with photographs of old rubber dolls and scenic or what he called anti-tourist images. In this sense he was almost a genius by the uniqueness of his vision, but a basic necrophilia tended to repel.

He had done an extraordinary photo of Max, topless and double-exposed into the wall of his studio, making Max look granite and very timeless. We made this into a postcard and we had the invitation to the show reproduced on the message side of the back in Max's handwriting. The salutation was slurred so it might be anyone. These we addressed to our mailing list and sent to René Lefebvre in Paris with instructions to mail them back. Things got muddled but everyone got a postcard from Max with a nice French stamp, postmarked from Paris the morning of the exhibition. Some people came to the opening just to find out how we managed this.

We escorted Max in our jeep from Sedona in tandem behind his Ford and trailer full of paintings. The Ford had been around for a long time and conked out every hour or so. Max would get out, lift the hood, and frown at the motor. It would always start up again under his gaze. He grew flowers this way too.

Our show was the first retrospective of Max Ernst ever held. It was composed of over three hundred pieces including drawings and collages. We borrowed wherever we could, Germany, France, England. It never occurred to us that anyone would refuse and, oddly, nobody did. Ernst lovers have always made up a sort of secret society of people who knew why they trusted each other.

Julien Levy lent the great *Vox Angelica* and other paintings he had. Iolas lent and Pierre Matisse lent. Walter Arensberg lent. Roland Penrose in London lent everything he had. I met him the next year at a Man Ray opening in Paris. An hour later we were on our way to the south of France with a friend, a mistress and an ex-wife, in one of those old black Citroëns that looked like a pair of banker's glasses. I remember we played group chess with one of Man Ray's magnetic sets passing from the front to the back seat.

Marie-Laure, La Vicomtesse de Noailles, lent her two gigantic bird monuments. She was one of the last salon keepers. I met her later in her salon, amid a garden of budding celebrities. I never managed a season ticket however.

The Museum of Modern Art lent.

Nobody asked credentials.

Allie Lewin lent *The Temptation of Saint Anthony*. Somewhere we got the *Rendezvous des Amis*. The Wadsworth Athenaeum lent their *Napoleon in the Wilderness*. The title comes from a very dirty story. We exhibited the entire originals of *Une semaine de bonté*, Max's seven visual novels done with collage on old steel engravings. A professor from an art academy gathered his class before these to prove that, contrary to some opinion, Max Ernst could really draw.

The cover of the catalogue was a naughty photograph of Dorothea sitting on the lap of Max's huge concrete sculpture he'd built in Sedona, *Capricorn*. Her hand listlessly rested on what some thought was the indecent item of the piece.

We published a book of Max's poems and collages with pages of personal homage which hadn't been hard to gather. A deluxe edition of twenty had a signed etching of Max's. We couldn't sell them and finally gave them back to Max against a painting. It didn't matter again, as our bookkeeper discovered we were trying to sell them under cost. We had the unhappiest bookkeeper on the West Coast anyway.

Max was in splendid form. Our visits to Sedona had been pilgrimages. We could savor Max and his wit and after long Arizona evenings even get some sleep. Max in Los Angeles was the next best thing to an orgy. He was loved and entertained and never felt like going to bed. I can only remember the days as a blur. We even tried going back to Sedona for some sleep.

This show was from a practicable point the greatest disaster of all because so much went into it. There was no appreciation.

Except from the kids.

A lad of about nine or ten wandered in one day and spent a long time looking at the pictures. Maybe he was the one who sold us the bird. I don't remember. The next day he came back with a friend and they both spent a long time looking at the pictures. Then there were four of them. Their numbers seemed to double every day. They didn't laugh or horse around. They looked quietly, seriously, profoundly mesmerized by the fantasy of Max Ernst. It was a mini version of the success we'd dreamed of.

We did know that we'd made unrecorded history. It was time to listen to the lamentations of the bookkeeper. His evidence could not be refuted. What the venture had cost in terms of rent, maintenance, salary, printing, postage, packing, shipping, insurance, liquor, and money suddenly was staggering. If we'd had business heads, we'd never have dared the project in the first place. There was nowhere further to go. No one wanted to buy our pies. In that sense we'd paid the price for the education.

It's different now. When I do return to California from time to time, the past is treated reverentially. I am rather respected and accused of having had foresight. It would be unfair or disillusioning to spill the beans that we really didn't know what we were doing at all. Unhappily, the brother-in-law died with an automobile and cannot share the belated credit. It seems better that I try to accept such admiration with modesty. The past is always a beautiful time.

About the Hare and the Tortoise but Mostly About the Hare

First published in French translation by Carolyn Breakspear as "Du lièvre et de la tortue et principalement du lièvre" in *Francis Picabia* (Galeries Nationales du Grand Palais, 1976)

The word *genius* annoys me. It is beyond definition, is used too loosely, and if it exists at all, applies to an excess of mental energy so far beyond the norm as to suggest that the possessor is something of a freak, like someone with two or three heads. Milhaud once told me that if a professional copyist started at the age of consent to copy all the works of Bach, he could not complete the job in his lifetime. I generally cite this example to suggest that the nature of time has changed that radically between now and then. But how do we explain the number of expensive works that Picasso was able to produce in his lifetime? Even the forgers have not been able to keep up with him. I'm not interested in the concept of genius.

Nor am I too impressed with who gets credit for discovering what. Simply because someone does something for the first time does not mean that he has invented or discovered anything. Points in time, history if you will (though this is another word I quibble with), make most inventions inevitable. The same applies to revolutions.

So it was with Dada. It has not even been established to anyone's satisfaction who found the word in the dictionary. Dada sprung up in different places, Barcelona, New York, Zurich, at about the same time through a kind of spontaneous generation with its own hippies and war protesters responding to the complacency and disillusionment of the time they were living in. It finally involved a considerable array of intelligent and talented people.

Few of these were ever accused of genius. They were eccentrics who were to be responsible for changing the face of modern art through calculated scandal.

In the hands of politicians eccentricity can be dangerous. In the hands of artists it is quite safe. There is a wistful competition among artists to paint a painting that could kill. Picasso is the only one I know who claimed success at this.

Francis Picabia and Marcel Duchamp were the two great poetic eccentrics of our time.

Picabia and Duchamp became friends in 1911.

Eccentrics have always been first in recognizing art, erasing all the efforts of historians, curators, critics. Usually they're collectors. Occasionally they are dealers. Witness Walter Arensberg, Katherine Dreier, Barnes, Eddy.

Picabia painted his *Caoutchouc* in Paris in the year 1909; Marcel Duchamp his *Coffee Grinder* in 1910. These are very similar conceptions. I seem to remember another like them by Serge Charchoune then from Barcelona, dated, I think, 1910. These were remarkable paintings in that they suggested machines to come.

In 1912 Picabia came into the orbit of Apollinaire, that year supposedly marking his first totally abstract work. In 1913 Picabia was in New York participating in the Armory Show and meeting Alfred Stieglitz and Marius de Zayas and most probably the great eccentric Arthur Cravan.

Picabia was fascinated with New York and considered it the only Cubist city in the world.

In 1914 he was drafted and in 1915 while on a posh foraging mission to the Caribbean (an assignment attained we would guess through family clout) he took French leave to New York to collaborate with Duchamp on *291*. He spent much of his time voyaging between New York, Barcelona, and Zurich, till allowed to return to Paris in 1919. Being well heeled, he could afford to travel during this period, when communication was difficult. Thus he became the carrier pigeon for the eccentric ideas of Dada.

More important he was the catalyst as well as an animator of the movement.

Today we know almost all that needs to be known about Duchamp. He has entered the Pantheon. He has been studied and written about by the scholars and critics. He has been exhibited internationally and in depth. His life and his work have been recognized. His imprint on his time is firmly established. Not only that, he lived to see it all happen, perhaps not against his will, but something to his surprise.

I'm a great one for knocking on the doors of those I most admire, figuring most artists don't resent others' interest in their work and that something about them may rub off on me. I have rarely been thrown out. What I have learned through the friendships I have made this way has enriched my life immeasurably. I did get to know Duchamp through this tactic for which I will ever be grateful.

I don't know why I never knocked on Picabia's door. He was older before an opportunity presented itself. By then there were rumors about his health. Also I felt an unusual shyness proportionate to the awe in which I held him. I shall forever regret it. I might of course have learned a little more about the prewar shenanigans. But worse, it frustrates to have to speculate when any personal contact would surely have helped to lift the lid for me.

Up till now so little has been known about Francis Picabia. While Duchamp was in many ways his own biographer, if not his own curator, Picabia was too impatient to care to drop any pebbles for the pursuing scholars. Most of his works are scattered, often unrecorded, in many cases unvalued. We know him through chronologies and incomplete prefaces. There is a surge of interest now, and a comprehensive biography by William Camfield of Rice University, long in preparation, will be appearing next year. There was an exhibition several years ago at the Guggenheim. There is this exhibition.[1] He did not live to know it would happen.

---

1. *Francis Picabia*, Galeries Nationales du Grand Palais, Paris (January 23–March 29, 1976).

To know Duchamp and not to know Picabia is to know but half the history. For these two are the Castor and the Pollux of Dada. The yin and the yang. Also the hare and the tortoise. The two great eccentrics who were as different as they were similar.

Duchamp wrote of Picabia in a preface for William Camfield's monograph for Schwartz's show: "As a lad of fourteen he joined the Impressionists and showed a great talent as *a young follower of an old movement . . .*" (The italics are mine.) One might say, "Speak for yourself, Marcel." In this context it should be noted that both artists also traveled the road of Cubism to where they were going. As for Abstraction, Duchamp moved quickly toward Conceptualism. *Object to Be Looked at With One Eye Only,*[2] being as close as he would come to anything really abstract.

Neither artist was averse to employing popular images. William Camfield points out rightfully that Pop had its own motivation. Such images were used by the Dadaists in context with their destructive purposes.

Further on in the same article Duchamp writes: "Between 1917 and 1924 the Dada movement, a metaphysical attempt toward irrationalism, offered little scope for painting. Yet Picabia in his paintings of that period showed great affinity with the Dada spirit." This could be a little damning with faint praise, except while both men represent most that we really remember as Dada, Georges Hugnet notes that in the formal phase of Dada there was always a Picabia–Duchamp spirit opposed to a Breton spirit or a Tzara spirit. Duchamp credits Picabia as not joining the club itself any more than he had. This might be a contradiction in light of Picabia's apparent identification with *391* but particularly in Picabia's case he maintained a Dada attitude toward Dada itself. Both men were too interested in moving on.

What André Salmon says of Picabia applies equally to Duchamp. "Whatever he does Mr. Picabia has the right to be studied as a true artist the more he denies art." The twins were here identical in motivation, freedom of poetic expression toward limitlessness.

---

2. *To Be Looked at (from the Other Side of the Glass) with One Eye, Close to, for Almost an Hour* (1918).

They were anti definable, criticizable, recognizable, respectable art. What they destroyed they put back together their own way for the benefit of the future.

What Henri-Pierre Roché says of Duchamp, "His greatest work was his use of time," also applies to Picabia. The greatest achievement for any creative person is to arrive where his personality, his life, is synonymous and indistinguishable from his work.

The similarities do not stop here but run on profoundly. They were both men of enormous humor which they each expressed or achieved their own way.

Duchamp, the tortoise, had a cerebral humor, inside jokes, inside himself at that. Mostly he structured elaborate puns which kept skipping on into the subconscious like flat stones on water. Duchamp didn't write any more than he had to as he didn't paint any more than he had to. His letters were more like telegrams. He wrote a good deal of criticism mostly for Katherine Dreier, avoiding at all costs being overtly negative. One always had to go looking for his humor, sometimes his disapproval or annoyance. In the preface already cited above, he carefully omits to mention Picabia's mechanical period and wipes out the era known as the monster period (personally, my favorite) thusly: ". . . he turned to paint for years watercolors of a strictly academic style representing Spanish girls in their native costumes." How could he not have known of these lovable paintings! But in the same piece he also pays Picabia profound compliments and in dealing with the transparent period he points out: "By a juxtaposition of transparent forms and colors the canvas would, so to speak, express the feeling of a third dimension without the aid of perspective." And, "Picabia, being very prolific, belongs to the type of artist who possesses the perfect tool: an indefatigable imagination."

Indeed it is hard to say what was the personal relationship between the two men. Duchamp never spoke of Picabia in my presence. Somewhere along the line there may have been a cooling. Picabia was given to practical jokes, another aspect of his humor, alas, something Duchamp would not have had patience with. Man Ray described one played on him, but years after it happened when he could laugh at it.

In the paintings or objects Duchamp, the tortoise, invariably hid his jokes in convoluted puns, verbal, often in the titles, or visual, so the works remained in a way puzzles to be solved.

The *Large Glass* was totally mythological in concept and to read it we have to learn the private science he invented for it, "meta-irony." The *Green Box* was its rosetta stone.[3] It was all an enormous serious joke.

Picabia, the hare's humor, was all from the belly. He too loved to make aphorisms, was certainly a master at it, and was not afraid to use outrageous puns. And like any good entertainer would sometimes go to great lengths to set them up. Duchamp was satisfied as long as they remained preposterous.

Unlike Duchamp, Picabia was as prolific in his writing as he was in his paintings.

Primarily his was a humor of attack. He was concerned with breaking up the ball game: war, sex, religion, conviction, consistency, love, other artists, himself. His tools were sarcasm and ridicule spread evenly with lavish imagination. When it was all over, there was to be only freedom apparent. Duchamp too sought freedom as his end but he had a horror of polemics.

Very little escapes the venom of Picabia's attack. At random:

Jesus Christ Jockey! Yes, he becomes the curiosity of crowds. He races, everyone bets on him. The results for the bettors: nothing.

Purity hides behind our sex.

Style is a dead leaf.

3.   *The Bride Stripped Bare by Her Bachelors, Even* (1934), commonly known as the *Green Box*.

Taste is fatiguing like good company.

Humorists are the worst idiots. They can only amuse those among you, dear readers, who accept to wear chastity belts.

Morality is the backbone of imbeciles.

I have a horror of the paintings of Cézanne, they bug me.

As a critic he behaved very much like Arthur Cravan the professional scandalizer, poet, and boxer, who upset a literary meeting in New York so successfully as to gain incarceration in Sing Sing for a week. In one of his handbills he liked to pass out, Cravan suggested that Marie Laurencin be publicly spanked. Picabia kept his tongue more in his cheek, the purpose being mostly to provoke.

Picabia was a prolific poet and I consider most of his writings poetry. It was a poetry of the outrageous which the titles almost suffice to illustrate: "Fifty-Two Mirrors," "Girl Born without a Mother" (also used as title for several paintings), "The Athlete of the Funeral Parlors," "Unique Eunuch," to cite a few.

Caravansérail, a fictionalized autobiographical odyssey of improbable episodes in settings only probable for Picabia, slanders about everyone he ever knew, including himself, and doubling as an anti-Surrealist manifesto. It could make one think of Jarry, an author Picabia steadfastly refused to read, which I suppose sheds some light on the nature of his vanity.

In the sense of contributing to the idea of humor being a necessary element of total expression in creative activity, he must be considered again to share the honors with Duchamp. Duchamp's *Mona Lisa's Mustache*[4] makes about the same statement as Picabia's stuffed monkey object, *Portrait of Cézanne–Renoir–Rembrandt–Still Lives*,[5] dated 1920. He often borrowed puns from Duchamp as in *The Double World*, 1919. For Duchamp such

4. *L.H.O.O.Q.* (1919).
5. *Tableau Dada* (1920).

irreverences were single gestures. For Picabia they were practically a way of life. Already in the Cubist works of 1912 and 1913 we suspect that something funny is afoot. The titles seem to ask us not to take them too seriously as either representational or nonrepresentational. All of what was going on in Duchamp's *Nude Descending a Staircase* and *Sad Young Man on a Train* is happening in Picabia's *Procession Seville* and *Figure triste*. What happens with Picabia is that he starts having more and more fun with the titles which tempts us to enter the picture more and more in search of esoteric happenings. When we get to *Girl Born without a Mother* we may realize that we have been looking at machines for some time back.

I do not believe the titles are random (though I admit one can be fooled as by Tanguy pulling words out of a hat). I feel I notice a personal poetic association of humorous myth with which Picabia is intentionally teasing us. The idea of a machine to perpetuate a memory (*This Thing Is Made to Perpetuate My Memory*, 1915) is a droll concept. The laughter sounds louder as we come to the mechanical objects and portraits where our minds as viewers are made to participate in recognizing of the objects or persons through a sense of humor that we didn't know we had.

The machines become more elaborate and/or more esoteric, also more formal, and again the inexplicable laughter mounts, laughing at something sinister as in *La Nuit espagnole*, 1922, with its subtitle, *Andalusian Blood*, or *The Animal Trainer*, 1923.

The optical paintings must clearly have been inspired by Duchamp's optical experiments which sought to achieve meaningless solutions to meaningless problems. According to Camfield, Picabia put his "optophones" to work converting "electrical energy into sexual energy." This is a process similar to much that happens in the *Large Glass* of Duchamp. Perhaps Picabia was chalking up a point of one-upmanship on Duchamp. Picabia's *Echelle optique*, 1922,[6] almost certainly involved a portrait of one

6.   Possibly a reference to *Optophone I* (1922) or *Optophone II* (c. 1922–25).

of Duchamp's optical machines, embroidered with feminine accoutrements.

Collage in the hands of an anti-artist can only be hilarious. Both Schwitters and Ernst (an anti-artist certainly at the time and forever a humorist) used collage to great effect to stimulate incongruous amusement or fear. Picabia in his monster period (a designation I have never thought much of applied to my favorite group of paintings) creates the greatest happiness when he goes into collage. It was his use of banal and vulgar materials which gave them their mystery and joy: tooth picks, drinking straws, buttons, feathers, et cetera.

As for the monsters, since I have to call them that, I revel in these paintings. I see them as double edged, on the one hand as ribald celebrations of love, on the other as boobs on classical themes. They are smallish portrait-sized paintings. As often as not they involve lovers embracing tenderly and clumsily as though trying to figure where the noses go. The jagged anarchy of the painting style is in tune to the rise of good clean sexual passion. These are violent and deliciously innocent paintings. Certainly they are the strongest, most courageous, and most individualistic of Picabia's entire output. I can think of no one of his contemporaries who treats affection as nicely as Picabia does in these monumental hymns to profane love. Duchamp's piece, the gentler version of the *Large Glass, Étant donnés,* in Philadelphia, remains intellectually clinical in comparison to Picabia's sweethearts. They are the half-hidden lovers waiting for the last bus that we so often stumble upon. The world does not exist beyond their touching of each other. The techniques of the later transparencies may have resulted in Picabia's attempt to achieve a further fusion of their embraces. They represent a sudden breakthrough for Picabia into what he really wanted to say about life being so instantaneously exciting. In so often choosing to borrow the structure of well-known classical paintings he achieves a timelessness to the highly charged passionate feelings he is depicting. When not embracing figures they are apt to be just women often dripping with longing.

The humor here is tender. Lovers do not care how ridiculous they look. Might we not call these something else than "monster" paintings.

Picabia took to working in Ripolin in order that his canvases appear not to be paintings; oil paintings felt museum dead to him once signed. He liked to go one step further from time to time and purposely make his painting so vulgar, so badly done as to affront all sensibilities. I'm thinking, for example, of *Portrait of Suzy Solidor*, 1933; *Deux Danseuses*, 1922; *Woman and Bulldog*, 1941 or 1942; others whenever we choose to recognize them as such. I wouldn't want to attack anyone's favorite paintings. Again I am tempted to compare early Pop art to these deliberate disasters. Certainly they were prophetic.

Picabia was a master draftsman and engraver as well as a competent Impressionist at an early age. But he had the power to undo his craft when it suited his needs.

I must confess the transparent paintings do not amuse me much, though technically they were probably inevitable. Transparency had been slowly but logically sneaking into the so-called "monster paintings." Until I read what Duchamp saw in them, I had very little understanding. I guess I expected to keep on laughing. I'm afraid we begin to laugh less and less with Picabia as the end of his life approached.

But one can talk of the funniest film ever committed to celluloid, *Entr'acte*. There was Duchamp playing chess with Man Ray, E. S. for Erik Satie, initials on a hearse along with those of F. P. The film is total anarchy ending with a chase scene that doesn't leave a dry pair of pants in the house.

There were the publications. *291* ran twelve issues from March 1914 to February 1915, in collaboration with Duchamp. *391* started in Barcelona in January of 1917, continued in New York, Zurich, and Paris through nineteen irregularly spaced issues. *391* has been called the mirror of Picabia and holds much promising material for his scholars. His entire attitude to life and arts are revealed there. Unfortunately a complete edition is difficult to come by. In 1920 there were two issues of *Cannibale*. The hare and the tortoise often collaborated but Duchamp would be the first to lose interest. It was a passion for Picabia to continue. But he had no patience to catalogue and no desire to be catalogued. Like Duchamp he expected to be unknown.

His passions were about equally divided between painting and his literary activities.

The hare and the tortoise treated their energy differently. Picabia could not know satisfaction. For him there was no yesterday and no tomorrow. People who react strongly know more anguish. For Picabia it was spending, gambling, drinking, womanizing, opium, fast cars, yachts, painting, writing, editing, manifesting. Duchamp boasted of masterful inactivity.

After perspective or say Impressionism it is impossible for an artist to continue as though perspective or Impressionism had not happened. These things simply became part of his vocabulary. If history does exist, its progress is geometric. From the automobile to the aircraft to the atom to the moon in two generations ain't bad. The first half of the twentieth century has known Impressionism, Fauvism, Cubism, Dadaism, Surrealism, Abstraction, Picabia, and Duchamp.

I have found it not feasible to discuss the hare without the tortoise. Only these two shared such an intensity of vision. The dust has not yet settled from their explosive passage. For both of them nothing was without significance. Between them they set the stage for the art we know today.

One final statement from Duchamp, again from the piece I've quoted throughout: "In his fifty years of painting, Picabia has constantly avoided adhering to any formula or wearing a badge. He could be called the greatest exponent of freedom in art, not only against academic slavery, but also against slavery to any given dogma."

Joseph Cornell

Originally published in *Joseph Cornell* (Leo Castelli Galllery / Richard
L. Feigen Company and James Corcoran Gallery, 1976)

I knew Joseph Cornell just a little bit and saw him only a few
times. To Julien Levy must go the credit for having discovered
him as an artist. I can only take credit for having responded
to him with a bang as early as about 1947.

As I remember, I met him as he was coming off an elevator
and I was leaving the old Hugo Gallery, where I'd been with
Iolas laying some groundwork for a gallery I was going to open
in Beverly Hills. He was carrying two shopping bags full of boxes
and Iolas must have introduced us, as I remember following
them back into the gallery. I saw what was in the shopping bags
and managed to buy an entire exhibition from Joseph—roughly
fifty pieces. I think the deal was consummated at a nearby ice
cream parlor. Cornell was gaunt and gray and shabby.

Being with him was like going down a rabbit hole, he was so
like his boxes. Afterward, it seemed like it would be years before
I would find my way back to wherever I left from that morning.
Just to converse with him, one had to leave the familiar world and
enter his. His world was very like Kafka's *Amerika*.

The California exhibition was an enormous failure. I know
it's bad syntax to qualify a word like failure, but it applied in
this case.

We'd designed a catalogue in what I considered to be Cornell
blue and white. We rented a white high-wheel bicycle from a
Hollywood prop rental and draped it in blue velvet. We displayed
the boxes on glass shelves with clay pipes liberally dispersed.

I couldn't restrain myself going one step further and plastering the walls and then even the ceiling with the blue and white catalogues. Finally I was convinced that I'd turned the gallery into something of a Cornell box.

What I didn't figure was that most of us spend our lives fighting the idea of going into a box. People came, but they just looked in through the door. I remember somebody snottily saying, "I thought this was an art gallery."

And it was really a very beautiful show. I would have bought it all myself except that I'd already bought it.

There was the American Rabbit quivering and waiting to be shot. There were the Taglioni Jewel Boxes, souvenirs of a great departed ballerina of whom it was said that she once danced boliki on the snow for brigands. Souvenirs too of Lucile Grahn, Alicia Markova, a homage to *Swan Lake*.

There were Soap Bubble Sets galore. There were books with cutout words or marbles in them seen through a window. There were butterflies occupying empty rooms. There were kaleidoscopes and boxes of multicolored sand. Round powder boxes too of the Nile (blue green) or Turkey full of tied-up bits of history pages to be assimilated like bonbons. There was Paolo and Francesca and Paul and Virginia necking secretly. There were the palaces with forests growing through their windows. There were the Pharmacy and the Beachcomber Bottles, the Thimble Garden for Alice in Wonderland and the Lobster Quadrille, the only hilarious piece I've ever known Cornell to do—boiled-red Coney Island celluloid lobsters in a mirrored chorus line. There was a paperweight of tight bound paper. There were pieces I almost don't remember anymore.

And no one would set foot in that room. I was stuck with a lot of Cornell boxes. Cornell wouldn't talk to me for three years afterward. He blamed the fiasco on my greed in doubling the prices he'd suggested—two hundred instead of one hundred dollars for the big ones.

The gallery failed a few months after that and I went to France to live out the disgrace. The Cornells went to sisters, cousins, and aunts, one of whom made lamps out of them.

I saw Joe a few more times after I was eventually forgiven. I remember a tea party at the Plaza. An attorney I knew from Chicago wanted to meet him and was a cautious collector. Cornell owned that he had an uncle who once got as far as Chicago. The attorney was the nondrinking kind and so they both needed their candies, pastries, and cakes for their blood sugar supply. All of a sudden there was a single cookie left. The conversation stopped completely (it hadn't really gotten anywhere much anyway), and I noticed that there were four hostile eyes glued on the last cookie. I could smell the tension. The lawyer man from Chicago finally swooped down on the cookie. When Joseph left, he took all the cubes in the sugar bowl, and I happen to know he didn't have a horse.

The last time l saw him was during a difficult time for him. He rather summoned me to Utopia Parkway as though he needed something from a friend. I'd always hoped to be invited there and while it had been mentioned before, this was the first and last visit to his domain. He wasn't there when I arrived, though sweets were laid out. He'd left word with his brother that I could browse in his attic until he returned.

In the attic everything was in meticulous order. The sun boxes stood in a line next to Hotel D'Étoiles next to the Soap Bubble Sets next to . . . Occasionally there'd be a shock and a surprise. Anyway, it was an attic very full of boxes.

There was no way of knowing there was going to be a Cornell. No art historian ever prophesied the coming of the box. André Breton did make six boxes during his wartime stay in New York, but they could have been collages—they didn't have to be boxes. Cornell's boxes had to be boxes. His films lack the containment of form, no matter how fascinating they are. I feel his collages stay collages.

To me the only novels worth reading are the Bible and *Moby Dick*. Channel 13 was after all able to run even *War and Peace* as a soap opera.

I think of Queequeg in *Moby Dick* cheerfully working on the coffin which made it possible for Ishmael to tell his tale.

I think of the stars of Cornell's theater—the Medici boy, Taglioni, his movie stars, his empty hotel rooms, the bird cage of the departed bird, Paolo and Francesca, Paul and Virginia, most of them gone to meet the maker. I see Joseph Cornell as our Queequeg, our little old coffin-maker. Beautiful boxes for beautiful things that don't come back.

In My Career as a Name-Dropper

Letter to Anne d'Harnoncourt
Philadelphia Museum of Art, November 4, 1987

Anne d'Harnoncourt
Philadelphia Museum of Art
Benjamin Franklin Parkway
Philadelphia, PA 19130

Dear Anne,

It's late for the apology I owe you. Let me assure you what happened has nothing to do with my reputation for being a hermit and a nonparticipator. I suppose I go on being like this.

I had been eagerly awaiting the trip and saw it as a chance to not only pay tribute to Marcel, but to marshal and express my own thoughts about art and the underground as I felt them as a disciple of Marcel's as I see myself to be. The times seemed perfect for what I would have had to say. I had made cursory notes but I expected discussion itself would have prompted me. I had prepared extreme and offensive statements and had hoped to present myself as a warrior of Marcel's.

I am and had been spending a great deal of time up here in Rochester. I am engaged to a lovely lady doctor who is a (second year) resident at a hospital up here. She is given very little time for us to be together and absolutely no time for her to go anywhere.

I was on my way to New York to pick up the Metroliner when something medical and severe happened.

Although I finally managed to shed most of my major vices a few years ago, the piper keeps sending bills.

I'm still trying to find out what it was that happened on my attempt to get to Philadelphia but it all floored me. There didn't seem to be enough air on this planet for me to breathe. I didn't seem to be able to function hardly at all either mentally or physically, and I was totally depressed. I finally came back here to Rochester with appointments to start the search for the cause of all this.

For no reason at all I woke up yesterday morning feeling like a human being again, and immediately started thinking about writing this letter. Before even that would have been too much for me.

And I can now express my sadness of an opportunity missed not only to see old friends, but to have been able to make a state-ment bringing my life work and thoughts together, for I still see myself as finishing my education on the road that Marcel had set me on.

To make for what my illness did not allow me to say I will somehow, some day have to write about Marcel and how he make [*sic*] me see today.

Sort of really just for the hell of it I'm enclosing the notes I would have brought with me had I been able to come. Marcel was an inspiration to anyone who gave their attention to him, not with his way but to their way.

This is a big regret rather than an apology because I would have been there had I not been as ill as I was.

With my regrets,
Bill CPLY

In my career as a name-dropper I probably planted the notion that Marcel Duchamp was my best friend. He was. This does not mean that I was his best friend, but whatever as they say these days, let the chips fall where they may.

I was ready to discover what I call the Dada Surrealist revolution in my quest for something meaningful after finding out how disillusioning a World War was. It wasn't fun but in its own way was quite hilarious, except it left one with nothing to believe in. Enter Dada and Surrealism to fill this vacuum. Briefly put I opened an art gallery in Beverly Hills and started collecting Surrealists in dead earnest.

Man Ray was my first acquisition. Poor Man got spread pretty thin. He was the only living Surrealist in the entire Los Angeles area. He claims Hollywood did not need him, that Hollywood was Surrealism enough for its own needs.

Man Ray arranged for me to meet Marcel. The procedure was easy enough. Duchamp had held out against the telephone longer than any human on record, but if you were willing to send him a telegram you might get a postcard back, and it was still the era of the penny postcard.

I was to meet him in the lobby of the Biltmore. It seemed that the Biltmore had more lobbies than guest rooms and it took hours to find him. To my abject apologies he answered that he often came to the Biltmore just to ride the elevators.

I remember I took him to lunch at Luchow's. Before they would seat him they made him borrow a jacket and tie from one of the waiters. Wanting to impress him I made fun of one of the paintings on the wall. He spent most of the lunchtime pointing out to me what was interesting about the painting.

Being able to use Marcel's name put a stop to my being thrown out of galleries, and I was able to be taken seriously enough to open my West Coast gallery with East Coast contacts.

When I insisted on recompensing him for his invaluable assistance he finally accepted a check cheerfully enough announcing enigmatically, "But I will win."

In those days he lived in a single room above a beauty parlor on 14th Street overlooking Union Square. I remember a bathtub, I think it was in the middle of the room. There was a chess table with clock timers, chess pieces knee-deep in tobacco, a single chair with an orange crate for the opposition to sit. There was a tangled ball of twine nailed to the walls.

Another favorite Duchamp story. The second time I met him I was troubled. My marriage was breaking. He seemed to know about it but never referred to it. But he talked about life in such a way as to undo much of my anxiety. Robert Lebel accused me of sentimentality for telling this story, but Pierre Roché wrote of leaving troubled friends with Marcel for just this kind of therapy.

I made it a point to see Marcel at least twice a year. I used to call it charging my batteries.

He taught me all I needed to know about painting, that painting was a thing to do. He never talked of good or bad in reference to art. Only it was unforgiveable to be a bore.

When I finally had an opportunity to show him what I did he told me only that I should continue. That was enough to dedicate me to my work.

I suppose what best reflects what Marcel taught me was my discovery that "Art is not furniture." Only that it is a piece of living. Something that one does without the need of time.

It was obvious to him and he was perhaps the first to recognize that once a finished work can become property it is time for art to disappear underground. He accomplished this with his urinal. He removed art from its media. It was Henri-Pierre Roché who said his art was his use of time. That seems to me as far underground as one need go.

To know Duchamp, it is only required that one be serious about living. He will satisfy the definition of any thinking man's philosophy. He satisfies the alchemist, the numerologist, his passion for chess is strangely unrelated to the necessity of winning. The fornicator is at the center of the universe which is totally around him or into her. He is the honorary doctor of pataphysics.

I've been asked to comment on how my familiarity with
his work has affected what I do myself. I think immediately of
the mural, the one called *Tu m' (emmerdes)*, now hanging at Yale
and which I first saw in the library of Katherine Dreier. I think
of the shattering of dimension that this work accomplishes.
Once past the restrictions of the academic three dimensions lies
the infinity of poetic dimension, the endless levels of existence
all experienced instantaneously. The image, the shadow of the
image, the object itself, the painted tear repaired by the real safety
pin, his own technique and the technique of the sign painter who
deigned to affix his pointing hand onto the stranger's canvas,
the choice of two hundred fifty colors painted as sample cards,
et cetera, et cetera. Et cetera forever. The game I play now to try
to capture, to round up as many dimensions as possible to cause
someone I don't know to spend time and not walk by my painting.

Today it seems that art cannot be above ground without
blushing. Those who wish to share catharsis with another may
never know that contact. Friends converse at openings with their
backs to the artist's work, and they will come again when next
there is a hanging. And no one else will see. No one else will ever
see. And there will [be] a price on every work.

I remember once that a Mr. Hoving once said on the airwaves
that he was convinced that forty percent of New York residents
were convinced they were not allowed into the Metropolitan
Museum.

I remember Marcel suggested that the most fascinating artist
today might be working somewhere in darkest Africa whence
we will never know about him.

He said many embarrassing things. Even his strongest disciple
allows that present society cannot conceivably spare anyone more
than fifteen minutes of its time.

But Duchamp does show us that we need not rely on
walls or pedestals or specially constructed safety deposit slots
in foreign banks.

Which accounts [for] that strange and eerie terror I experienced on discovering that I had once executed a work of art presently owned by only a bank.[1]

1. In margin on page 4 of original letter: "He always managed to ensure that his work should not be for sale—no profit / Monte Carlo venture[:] to break even[,] not to beat wheel."

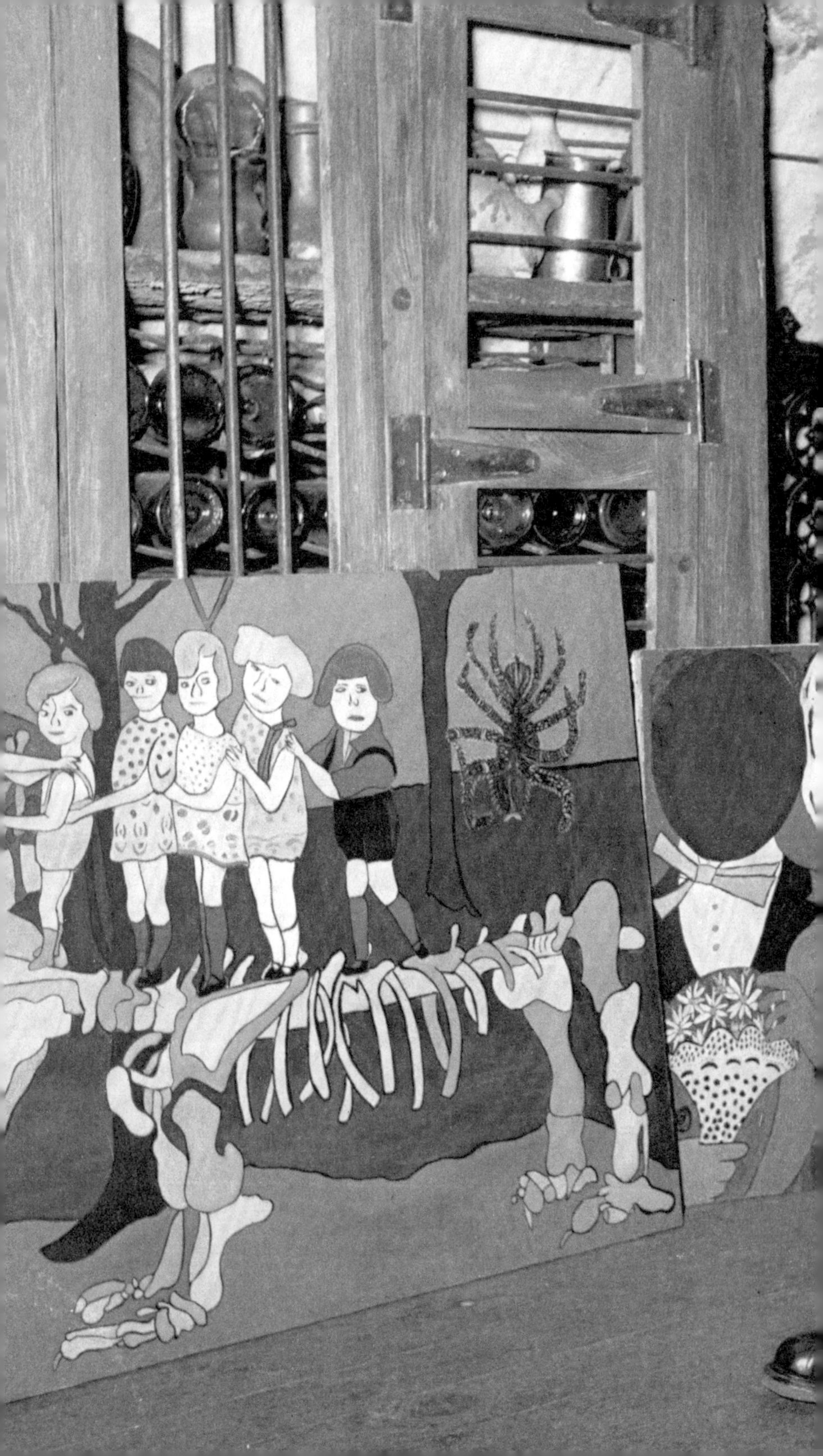

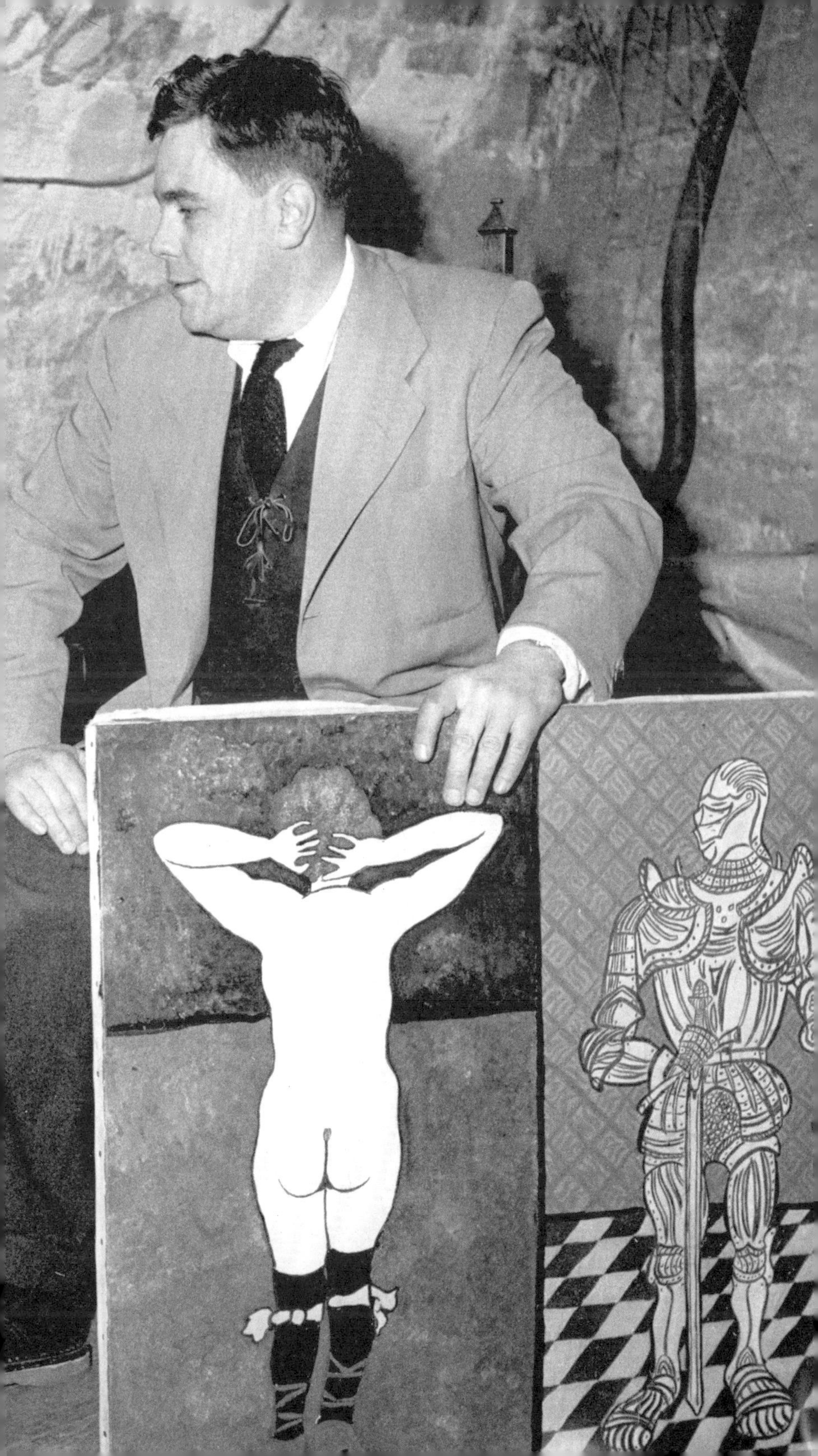

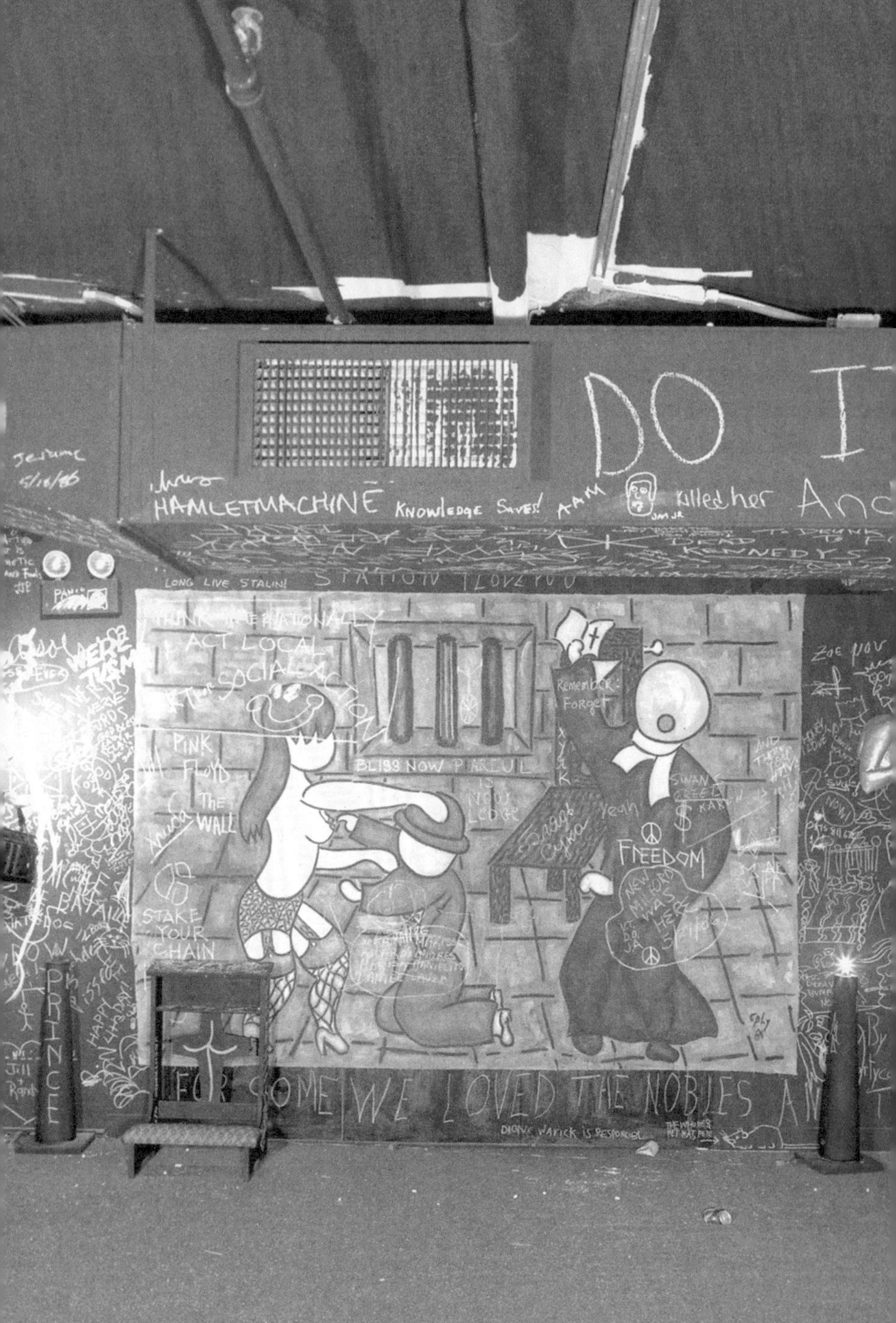

Jerome
5/10/86
HAMLETMACHINE KNOWLEDGE SAVES! AAM killed her
DO I
LONG LIVE STALIN! STATION I LOVE YOU
THINK INTERNATIONALLY
ACT LOCAL
SOCIAL ACTION
PINK
FLOYD
THE
WALL
STAKE
YOUR
CHAIN
BLISS NOW PARTIAL
IS
NOW
LEDGE
Remember
Forget
yeah
FREEDOM
NEW
MILFORD
WAS
HERE
PANIC
WE'RE
FOR SOME WE LOVED THE NOBLES
DIONNE WARICK IS RESTORED

II. Interviews, Texts, and Letters

Excerpts from Oral History Interview with William Nelson Copley

Paul Cummings, January 1969
Smithsonian Archives of American Art

PC: You were born in New York City.

WC: Actually, yes.

PC: But I always associate you with California.

WC: Well, I was an adopted child. And I think at the time I was adopted my father was in Congress, was a member from Washington [DC] for a few years. And I grew up in Illinois till I was about ten. And then when my mother died my father moved to California. And I got sent to see, I got sent—nobody asked me–I got sent to Andover and Yale.

PC: How did you like Andover?

WC: I hated it. I didn't like Yale very much either because I didn't feel I had any choice in the matter anyway and my father was of the class of 1887, was always having reunions, and was a very strong personality. And he felt that I should be a Yale man. So I was at Yale for three years and was a very bad student. I had one art course which was on Saturday mornings, the only class I had on Saturday morning, so I never saw any art. You know, they turn out the lights, start the slides, and I'd sleep it off.

PC: Who was teaching that, do you remember?

WC: Yes, I think it was George Heard Hamilton. That just might get me in trouble. So when the war came I wasn't doing terribly well. And I had a beautiful draft number—609.

PC: How in the world did you get such an exclusive number?

WC: I don't know. I usually do very badly on lotteries. But on this one I did pretty good. I got drafted very early. The Army and Yale sort of talked it out and thought it was the best solution to the whole thing. I had a few months to go when the war broke out. So I was actually in the Army almost four years. I was overseas most of the time.

PC: What did you do?

WC: Well, I started off in an anti-aircraft outfit. Then I managed to break my arm and I got put in an MP company. That bored me so much I volunteered for combat and got sent to Italy. And finally I got rotated home because I had gone overseas so early and I had been drafted so early. So I got rotated home and got out of the Army. But I never, never looked at a picture in my life until I was out of the Army. And when I got out of the Army I didn't know what do with myself. I first got mixed up in politics, which I found rather boring.

PC: Before we get into all this tell me some more about your family. You've lived in all these places, you know.

WC: My father was a newspaper publisher. He had been in Congress for twelve years then. Before that he'd been in the utility business and retired. And then got bored and went into the news-paper business.

PC: That was a California paper—right?

WC: California and Illinois both, yes. I worked for the paper
for about a year. The whole idea was that I was going to start
at the bottom and work up and sort of take over with my
brother. But—well, our politics differed. And it was about that
time I got interested not in painting but in writing. I wrote my
war novel—which I guess everybody else did. And then I met
up with a girl who had a brother-in-law. And I married the girl.
And the brother-in-law got me interested in Surrealism.

PC: Who is he?

WC: John Ployardt.

PC: Oh, he's the one you had the gallery with.

WC: I had the gallery with him. Actually he died last month
in an automobile accident.

PC: Oh, really?

WC: But he taught me everything I knew really. He had a very
engaging personality. And I was quick to pick it up. So I got
a very complete Surrealist background in a very short period
of time. And then of course learned much more after we had
the gallery. We showed Magritte, Tanguy, Joseph Cornell,
Man Ray, Matta, and Max Ernst in that order. And I think I sold
two pictures. I was trying to sell Cornell for $200. Just couldn't
do it. So I just went out of business. And about that time I got
divorced and I went to Paris—well, I came back for one year—
I lived in Paris for about twelve or thirteen years. Where I
just painted.

PC: I want to get some more early things. We're jumping ahead.
You have—what?—one brother?

WC: Yes.

PC: No sisters?

WC: I had a half-sister.

PC: Were you a close family?

WC: No, we weren't really terribly close. None of us were blood-related. Though we had more or less identical environments there wasn't any real closeness. Well, he went Right and I went further Left, you know. We never really came to any agreement. So it was impossible to think of working on the newspapers. I got out of that very early.

PC: Were you interested in writing when you were young?

WC: I always had been actually, yes.

PC: Any particular writers that interested you?

WC: Well, in those days we were raised on the Victorians. Which I adored, I must say. And I think English is the only course I ever passed.

[. . .]

PC: Were there any favorite authors that you remember?

WC: Of course Conrad I adored. And in those days I adored poetry.

PC: Oh, really? Could be the seeds of Surrealism.

WC: Yes. Emily Dickinson was my favorite for a long time. And of course Poe. I actually adored Poe. And a few other poets. Poe started a lot of things that I wasn't aware of.

[. . .]

PC: You didn't study painting ever, did you?

WC: Never studied it, no. My painting all developed just through the painters I knew. Actually we were talking about it today. It was Duchamp and Max Ernst who encouraged me to continue painting. I really started painting as what I thought was an exercise to writing. Because I had read Joyce and decided that my writing was not sufficiently visual. And I thought that by painting I could sharpen my visual perception and be able to transmit that into my writing. And once I got started painting I never returned to writing really except for a brief period of journalism.

PC: When you started painting, were you trying to do very realistic things? Or poetic things? Or how would you describe it?

WC: Well, when I started painting first I was just trying to make a painting, you see, which seemed like a very difficult thing to do. And these paintings were jumped upon as primitives. I was told that they were good and that I should do more of them—which did encourage me. And then meeting people like Max and Marcel and eventually some of the others; Man Ray was a great friend of mind in those days. I began to see the possibility of poetry and painting. Poetry and of course humor in painting are the areas I'm really most interested in.

PC: Let's see, you were in the Army, and you came out, and you started painting in what—about 1946? 1947? Or something like that?

WC: 1946, yes.

PC: Was that when you met Ployardt?

WC: Just after I met him, yes.

[. . .]

PC: Were you interested in—or are you still interested in the literary aspects of Surrealism?

WC: Well, I always call it poetic. Because I don't believe it's literary. I believe it's poetic.

PC: How do you differentiate it?

WC: Well, for me it's the difference between a simile and a metaphor. A painting for me is a metaphor. I mean, it's a poetic metaphor rather than a poetic simile which it might be if it were literary.

PC: Oh, I see.

WC: Magritte is the best example of this, of course. The way I was taught in high school "a woman is like a rose" is a simile; and "a woman is a rose" is a metaphor. But Magritte for me is the master of the metaphor, to answer this question properly.

[. . .]

PC: What do you think is the difference between the New York and the Paris art scene since you've been in both?

WC: Of course there has been an almost total stop in Paris in

the sense of its activity. It's taking up again a little bit now.
But still it's nowhere near as exciting as it is here. But what
I do think—and it's a terrible thing to say—I do think that the
atmosphere of New York forces you to feel you have to make
it. And Paris I think traditionally was the place you went to
when you didn't want to make it. People went to Paris to paint,
to get away from their rich families, you know, and live in
cafés and paint and be beatniks.

PC: I think that Paris never really had that commercial drive and
never quite attained that much ambition, whereas New York is
I think concerned with ambition.

WC: Yes. It's interesting to see the revolt among the kids who are
trying very hard to paint without ambition. My son is a painter
and he's gone off to the desert with a friend of his—they're
going to dig trenches in the desert and photograph them from
the air. What they're accomplishing, of course, is a work of art
that cannot be sold. A lot of kids are thinking in these terms
and working in these terms, which I think is a reaction against
the pressure.

PC: Of making a marketable product, that kind of thing.

WC: Yes.

PC: That's very interesting because, you know, Paris still has
always been a center for dealing. For centuries it's been a place
to buy and sell, trade pictures, and the auctions, and all that
kind of thing.

WC: Even there it's quieted down. I mean London has replaced
it as the big auction center.

PC: Why do you think that's happened to Paris?

WC: I think probably what happened was that at a certain point they were trying to skyrocket everything in Paris. I think they went past a level where people would pay and everybody stopped buying at once, overnight. And it never seemed to revive.

PC: I know. It's never been able to get going after that.

WC: Yes. And that was at the height of what they call the *tachisme* and there were all sorts of very chic young painters who were being entertained and getting very high prices and the level was being pushed and pushed and pushed. I think everything went too high too fast. And people just stopped buying overnight.

PC: Do you think that will happen, or is happening here? Because some young people are getting fantastic prices.

WC: I really don't know what's happening here because I've been sort of organizing my life in the last two years. I haven't been painting, and I haven't been on the scene or going to galleries or museums even. So I'm out of it.

PC: Did you follow the shows in Paris when you were there other than the Surrealist?

WC: Yes. Because you always went to each other's shows. It was unthinkable not to.

PC: It used to be that way here with the abstract expressionists but now it seems to be changing.

WC: Oh, yes. I don't think it's that way at all anymore.

PC: The great names don't appear for the young guys' shows very often anymore. Ten years ago you'd meet half a dozen.

WC: Yes. It was a social duty almost.

PC: And they all lived here. Now they live in Woodstock or East Hampton or Southampton, or they're away teaching for six months at a university. And the whole social milieu has changed.

WC: Yes. And then of course a thing you can't forget is the population explosion being a large part of it. There are an awful lot more painters around than there used to [be]. An awful lot of kids that are a hell of a lot better than they ought to be. There is a lot of good work around.

PC: Why do you say they're better than they should be?

WC: Well, you just don't expect them to be that good. You know I had this magazine for the last year. And kids were coming to me every day and some were quite young.

PC: How did that whole thing grow up and get going—The Letter Edged in Black Press?

WC: There again, it came the way the gallery came, from drinking a lot of beer in the summertime and kicking ideas around. And one day we said let's do it.

PC: I'm very interested in that. I've seen the first two. The other two I haven't seen. There are four aren't there?

WC: There were six.

PC: Then there are two I've seen and four I haven't.

WC: They were meant to come out every two months. And then of course the same thing happened that happened in my gallery. I just got scared after about the fourth issue because I was spending a lot and nothing was coming in.

PC: Well, they were very complex.

WC: They were complex.

PC: How did you get the portfolio idea?

WC: Well, it was the idea of keeping the work individual art, you see. We didn't want to editorialize at all. We didn't want any critical comment. I wanted something that would just open up and be full of what was going on.

PC: Like a portable exhibition in a museum?

WC: Yes. With no comment. And that seemed the best way to do it.

PC: Who was involved in that with you?

WC: Well, there was Dimitri Petrov who was an awfully good painter in the forties, and never really painted enough. But he had a very good background in Surrealism and a mentality that was rather close to mine, so that we were able to work together terribly well. And he had spent a lot of time on Madison Avenue so that he knew the techniques which I of course had no knowledge of whatsoever. And then I got a lot of help from Sherwood Press. And then sometimes we'd just have to shop around until we could find somebody who would do the impossible. We were always looking for the impossible at that point.

PC: That's what makes it much more fun.

WC: Yes.

PC: How did you get the name for it—The Letter Edged in Black Press?

WC: It came from the lawyer. We wanted a name that would be sufficiently surprising. We tried a few and we came up with that one.

PC: There was *S.M.S.* or something else?

WC: Yes. *S.M.S.* is what we called the magazine. It was The Letter Edged in Black Press Incorporated. And the *S.M.S.* really had no particular meaning except between the two of us, which was supposed to mean *Shit Must Stop*. It was a terribly foolhardy adventure. I was between marriages, unable to paint, and looking for something to do. And I enjoyed it. The worst thing I feel about it is that I lost a good job. Because I liked it and liked doing it. But getting back to the kids, I was quite amazed. If you see the issues there's a lot of—they're very young and they just walk in and show me their material. And it was invariably of interest. I'll never forget one time there was a beautiful tall brunette who walked in with a big portfolio under arm. And she just stood in the doorway. I said, "And what do you do?" She said, "I do pornography." It was great pornography. But I did see a lot of very good work by young people just through having the magazine. I was quite surprised.

[. . .]

PC: How was your interest in humor—because you just had mentioned that a while ago about using humor and having it in painting?

WC: Well, my first contacts with the Surrealists were Man Ray, Max Ernst, and Marcel, who I think are the three greatest humorists around, you know. Marcel's humor is one kind of humor. Max's is another. And mine is another. My humor applies to the—what I like to say is the battle of the sexes. Sort of the impossibility of men and women to get together no matter how much they would like to. I don't know, it just happens to be the way I feel. I don't think about it very much. But I never seem to come up with anything else.

PC: I was looking through the Stedelijk Museum catalogue yesterday and I noticed there were some very interesting things. They'd have like a comic page where they'd have little boxes and a story. And one of the things that amused me was that they would go from French to English. You know, there'd be French here and English there, or a French sign and English words. Do you notice any difference, or does that just happen as you go along that—

WC: Well, you see, it's definitely true that some things are funnier in English than they are in French and vice versa. Duchamp was very well aware of this. Certain of his puns are totally untranslatable. Or they may be translatable but they still don't have the impact in translation because there'll be a nuance, or maybe just through French usage that will not translate or will not come across.

[. . .]

PC: But do you always make drawings for the paintings?

WC: I do now. I never used to. Well, I haven't painted for two years now. But as of the three years before that I would draw for three months, two months before I started to paint. I may not paint directly from my drawings but I find it necessary to have gone through the period of drawing to get myself in the mood for the painting—and usually the paintings have a common theme. Before I did the Service,[1] for instance, I did the American Ballad. And I find that drawing helps me more than anything else. The only reason I didn't draw more before was that there were two things that really frightened me; one is writing and one is drawing. Although I consider myself a fairly good writer, I hated it, it frightens me. And I never did learn to draw until I finally made myself learn. And now I feel that I've taught myself to draw but that was an effort I put off for a long time just out of laziness.

PC: What's the quality about it that bothers you, would you say?

WC: It's hard work. It's just like when I went to school. I didn't want to work.

PC: How did you hit upon Robert W. Service and the Yukon business?

WC: Well, I remembered it as a kid, you know. A friend of mine used to read it to me and those images stuck in my mind. It was Cliff Westermann who said to me once, "You should illustrate Robert W. Service." And this sort of cooked in my mind for about a year. And kept coming back.

PC: How in the world did he bring that up?

WC: I don't know. I can understand it coming from Cliff because I'm sure that Cliff Westermann probably sees Service just about the way I do, a man with a remarkable sense of imagery and very limited intellect. Which is a perfect combination for me who—I'm not really interested in intellectualism in either writing or painting.

1. Robert William Service (1874–1958). Service's writing was used as source material for a series of paintings by Copley in 1966–67.

PC: How would you define your interest in, say, writing? Since you're not interested in intellectualism, what does interest you then?

WC: I think the personal side. The sentimentality. I like to say warm things. I don't like to analyze. I don't think I have an analytical mind. I like to leave that to other people. I like to remark on the intensity of life but I don't want to take it apart into little pieces. I just don't have that kind of mentality.

PC: Is it similar in painting too?

WC: I think so, yes. Otherwise I would be painting pretty pictures. Which I've never really wanted to do.

PC: Have you ever been interested in abstract painting? Nonfigurative painting?

WC: Never. Never. Never in the least. Never for a moment.

PC: But your paintings have always been very flat and the space has never been deep space.

WC: No perspective. Because I don't know perspective. Matta was out at my house one weekend and I said to him, "Would you teach me perspective?" Because nobody knows perspective better than Matta and nobody is more articulate than he is. He said, "Yes. We'll go out to your studio in the morning." So we went out in the morning and he picked up a piece of charcoal and started to draw on my wall. Then he put the piece of charcoal down and said, "No, I'm not going to do it." And walked out. Because he didn't think I should do it. He thought he would be doing me more of a disservice than anything else.

[. . .]

PC: How would you describe Duchamp? Since you knew him for a long time. What kind of a person was he for you?

WC: Well, I would have to say a saint, you know. He was certainly the most inspirational person I've ever known. He was a person who knew how to live more than anybody else. He knew how not to worry, how not to be upset. He knew how to get through life pleasantly. Nothing was a problem for him. And I don't want to quote myself on things I've written. I always needed to see Duchamp, say, every three months if possible. Because I'd always come away with a stronger feeling about myself. He could somehow inject you with confidence and make things that seemed to be disturbing be ridiculous.

PC: In what way? You know that's a magical quality to have.

WC: Well, it was magical. It had to do with his philosophy that he himself was able to live by so well. I don't know if you saw the little piece I did for the *New York Times* when he died, which is very much a capsule of how I felt about him.

[. . .]

PC: One thing I've always been curious about, which is just an observation, is that in so many of your paintings the people have no faces or they're circular images or something.

WC: Yes. Well, that's very simple. I never had any luck drawing faces anyway. And so one day I was looking at something I was working on before I put the face in, and I thought, what will I need a face for anyway? Since I am only interested in men and women and the relationship between them, why do they need faces?

PC: So it's general rather than specific?

WC: Yes. I'm very happy to give up painting faces, which
I never learned to do.

PC: Well, you really are completely self-taught then?

WC: Yes. I've never studied with anyone.

PC: Do you think that the painting as opposed to writing—or
parallel to the writing, rather—is involved with a drive to
communicate? Or don't you feel painting is involved with that?

WC: I feel painting is for myself—this is just myself speaking—
painting for me is directly concerned with communication.
Actual communication of poetry. I always consider painting
and poetry synonymous.

[. . .]

PC: Do you think that the fact that you've lived in Europe all
that time had a great influence on your painting, the imagery
or the content of it?

WC: Certainly. I think any environment gets to your work right
away. I was in Mexico one time. It almost destroyed me. I was
surrounded by Mexican colors and Mexican light and it was just
too much for me. Too much for my palette. Or I spent a summer
in Venice because I had the children with me and you know all
the houses around there are pink or blue or soft pastel colors.
And I just didn't know where I was.

PC: Most of your things have been monochrome, haven't they?

WC: Particularly since I've been in New York I've done a lot
of monochrome.

PC: Why is that? New York is a gray city?

WC: Well, Paris is a gray city. I got used to it. And I like
gray cities because you can invent your own color. In colorful
cities the colors are on top of you. But I'm also very interested
in color. I'm interested in the dimensions of color, not the
picking-up of color, not painting Venice or Mexico. But I spend
an awful lot of time on color. And then it occurred to me
that if you have a drawing and the drawing isn't perfect you
have a perfect drawing. If you start a painting the painting will
not be perfect until it is perfect. Which means the colors have
to be just as right as the drawing has to be right in a drawing.
I almost say this eliminates the difference between painting and
drawing. Because if your colors are perfect nobody is going
to notice them particularly.

PC: Oh, the image is there and it works.

WC: Yes.

PC: Were you ever interested in color as a thing?

WC: Yes, I am. If I'm painting I won't give up until I feel
I've achieved perfection. And I began working on my palette.
But for about the last ten years I've worked exclusively in
glazes. The greatest thing that has happened to me has been
acrylics. Because before I used to have to work on ten pictures
at a time and let the glazes dry. And now I can just work a
picture through.

PC: You like acrylics then?

WC: Yes. I love them. But I don't use them the way New York painters use them. I mean, I use them the way I always use oil paint. I use them on canvas and not on cotton. I'm not interested in pure color areas. I find it's the greatest stuff in the world to glaze with. And on paper it's fantastic.

PC: Well, you've used all kinds of materials like lace and things in pictures.

WC: Yes. I've had lace periods and things like that.

PC: Do you still use different materials?

WC: Well, I haven't recently. I haven't painted for two years now. And I have *no idea* what I'm going to do next.

PC: How did you get involved with the lace?

WC: Well, it suddenly occurred to me, you see, that almost every material has connotation, poetic connotation. Look at that fur there, you see. And then getting into this masculine–feminine business again I said now what is the material that has the strongest female connotation. Obviously black lace. Then I had to find the material that would have the strongest male connotation. And so I decided on either corduroy or denim. So my interest in materials, you see, is purely connotative. Because I think it can give a dimension. But it's a poetic dimension.

[. . .]

Project for a Dictionary of Platitudes

Originally published in *CPLY* (Alexander Iolas Gallery, 1970)

WHEN I FIND MYSELF TALKING ABOUT ART IT MEANS I AM NOT
WORKING, ALWAYS A BAD SIGN.

THERE ARE NO ARTISTS, THERE ARE ONLY POETS EVEN IF THEY
ONLY MAKE MUD HUTS OR POEMS.

THERE ARE SECRET POETS LIKE THERE ARE SECRET DRINKERS.

A FLASH OF FUR WILL MOTIVATE A POET FOREVER. THIS I KNOW
TO BE TRUE.

MAN RAY SPEAKS OF A PAINTBRUSH WHERE THE HAIR IS ON THE
WRONG END; THUS HANGED MEN DIE WITH ERECTIONS.

POETS ARE THE LAZIEST PEOPLE IN THE WORLD BUT THEY MUST
ALWAYS FIND THEIR MR. LIVINGSTON I PRESUME.

I THINK POETS ARE NICER THAN OTHER PEOPLE BUT IT TAKES
LONGER TO FIND THIS OUT.

I FORGET WHO SAID THERE IS NOTHING NEW UNDER THE SUN.
OF COURSE THERE ISN'T. EVEN I COULD HAVE SAID THIS.

THERE IS NOTHING MORE BANAL THAN FURNITURE. AND YET IT
IS SO OFTEN CONFUSED WITH ART.

PAINTING I FEEL IS MAN'S CONCERN WITH WOMEN. MEN LOOK, WOMEN TOUCH SCULPTURE.

RELIGION IS A WEEKLY WAY OF BEING REMINDED OF OUR OWN MORTALITY. MAYBE POETRY IS SOMETHING ELSE.

THERE ALWAYS SEEMS TO BE TOO MUCH SELF-SATISFACTION IN CLEVERNESS. WE ALL FEEL IT. THIS IS A DAILY REMINDER OF OUR OWN MORTALITY.

TO THE POET THE ONLY MEDIUM OF EXCHANGE IS TIME.

THE MOST BEAUTIFUL POETIC STATEMENT IS METAPHOR. METAPHOR IS [A] LIE AS ANY IRISHMAN WILL TELL YOU.

THE FOURTH DIMENSION IS COITUS, NOT SAID BY ME BUT BY MARCEL DUCHAMP. OF COURSE, HE'S RIGHT, IF YOU THINK ABOUT IT.

I HAVE A VERY DIRTY MIND. IT HAS BROUGHT ME NEITHER SUCCESS NOR FAILURE.

WOMEN HAVE SHOPPING MUSCLES.

THERE IS MALE LOGIC AND FEMALE LOGIC. BOTH MANAGE TO BE VALID BY UNDOING THE OTHER.

THERE CAN BE NOTHING MORE BEAUTIFUL THAN TOTAL INSANITY ONCE IT IS ACHIEVED. WE MUST WAIT A LONG TIME FOR THE SECOND COMING.

I DON'T KNOW ANYTHING ABOUT ART, I ONLY KNOW WHAT I LIKE. "GOD PROTECT PEOPLE WHO STILL DARE SAY THIS."

A BANKER, A LAWYER, A DOCTOR, AND A MAN WHO MAKES OARLOCKS FOR GONDOLAS HAVE ALL INSISTED TO ME THEY WERE ARTISTS. I HAVE

NOT YET FOUND OUT HOW TO DISPUTE THEM BUT I AM WORKING AT IT.

GENIUS IS PROBABLY A MATTER OF ENERGY, THUS GENIUSES ARE
PROBABLY FREAKS WITH MORE ENERGY THAN THE REST OF US. I AM
NOT THE FIRST TO COMPLAIN OF THIS.

PICASSO IS A GYPSY WHO LIKES TO POSE FOR PHOTOGRAPHS AND
LISTEN TO HIMSELF TALK. HE APPEARS TO BE A GENIUS AND I MAY BE
THE FIRST TO COMPLAIN ABOUT THIS.

I UNDERSTAND THAT AS A HUNTER THEODORE ROOSEVELT FOUND
OUT THAT THE AFRICAN NATIVES COULD NOT READ PHOTOGRAPHS
WHICH HE TOOK THE TROUBLE TO TRANSPORT WITH HIM IN ORDER
TO IDENTIFY PREY.

I PAINT BECAUSE I CANNOT MAKE A LIVING AND VICE VERSA. SO FAR
NOBODY FEELS SORRY FOR ME ON THIS SCORE.

THE MARRIAGE OF ART AND TECHNOLOGY IS NOT SUFFICIENTLY
INCESTUOUS TO BE VALID.

MAX ERNST DOES NOT LIKE NAIVE PAINTING. HE BELIEVES IN A
SECOND NAÏVETÉ WHICH I INTERPRET AS THE CIRCUMNAVIGATION
OF ONE'S LIFE.

I CANNOT THINK OF ANY GAMES OR DIRTY JOKES OF MY OWN
INVENTION. THIS WORRIES ME.

THE CASE OF DE CHIRICO HAS ALWAYS INTRIGUED ME. IS IT MADNESS
TO PAINT OR IS IT MADNESS TO KNOW HOW TO?

HANS RICHTER HAS DESCRIBED SO WELL MARCEL DUCHAMP'S
UNDERSTANDING THAT DEATH DOES NOT OCCUR BECAUSE THERE
CAN BE NO REALIZATION OF IT.

SALVADOR DALÍ STOPPED PAINTING WHEN HE BECAME
RONALD REAGAN.

PRESIDENT EISENHOWER MAY HAVE BEEN THE GREATEST PAINTER
TO EVER INHABIT THE WHITE HOUSE.

RENÉ MAGRITTE ONCE FILMED A BANANA BEING EATEN BACKWARDS.
BY REVERSING THE FILM.

I SHALL NEVER FORGIVE ANDY WARHOL FOR PAINTING THE
MONA LISA.

ONE OF THE BLESSINGS OF OUR TIME IS ROY LICHTENSTEIN'S MEASLES.

I HAVE ALWAYS WANTED TO GIVE BARNETT NEWMAN A PING-PONG
BALL.

I HAVE BEEN SEEKING ALL MY LIFE FOR THE RIGHT PUN
ON MOTHERWELL.

POETS ARE ALWAYS SNUGGLY BURIED IN TIME FOR THE REVOLUTION.

CPLY: An Interview by Sam Hunter

Originally published in *CPLY: X-Rated* (New York Cultural
Center, 1974)

Sam Hunter: In view of the obvious focus of your current
exhibition on erotic subject matter, what do you think the
differences are between eroticism and pornography?

William Copley: It's a question of generation. My last exhibitions in which I used mail order objects exclusively expressed a
hidden pornography. I say pornography because I am seriously
concerned with the distinction between pornography and
eroticism. It's easy to hide pornography in objects. But in this
particular exhibition I decided to take the bull by the horns. For
me, it's a very simple thing: pornography has to do with repression, and eroticism with fantasy. When our generation is dead,
there will be no more pornography.

The fact is pornography has to do with the way we were
sat upon as children: sat upon sexually. In my home there could
be no reference to anything physical. I was sent to a boys' gram-
mar school, prep school, then to Yale—before they let girls in—
and finally to war, where I wound up in the desert. It took me
a long time to find out what a girl was.

It's possible that this exhibition is an attempt at self-therapy.
I'm jealous of these kids that go to school today and have
female roommates . . .

SH: Clearly then, an important motive for this show is personal.
Do you think your new work can also be fairly characterized as

satire, as an ironic comment on the sexualization and distortion of so many aspects of American life especially in the realm of pop culture?

WC: I'm trying to stop all that. I think that every exhibition that I have had until now was a form of satire. I'm not trying to unsatirize, but I am attempting to break through the barrier of pornography into the area of joy. It hasn't been easy.

When I had an exhibition in Paris, people I knew who felt rather sympathetic toward me said, "Mr. Copley, you don't like people." And I said, "Go back and look at every picture carefully." They went back and looked at every picture carefully. They took about an hour. They came back to me and said, "Mr. Copley, you really don't like people, do you?"

SH: You once said you were trying to find a balance between form and humor, linking this idea to Joyce and others in art and literature. I also recall that you said the Surrealists (Max Ernst and Duchamp in particular) were the only artists who achieved that kind of balance you are seeking. In these new works I find some of the same old engaging wit and irony despite the more explicit erotic themes. Is this a result of your having spent so much time in Europe? And, just to complicate matters, may I also ask if the impact of New York, of 42nd Street and Times Square, have not liberated you in ways that weren't possible when you lived in Paris?

WC: Having lived in Europe for a long time, and having lived now in New York for a long time, too, I have come to the conclusion that Americans tend to be overly conscious of Europeans. A painter is a painter, and, as Duchamp used to say, the greatest painter in the world may be somewhere in Africa and we will never know about it. The whole thing about European and American painting is terribly overplayed. The only reason we have American painting is because some Europeans came here as refugees and inspired younger artists. Earlier, they were painting ash cans; they suddenly decided there would be American art with a capital "A." I have nothing against that, but they did take a step backwards in trying to make sure that they would not be Europeans. Art is not national, it's universal. We've lost time in trying to pick our nationalities.

SH: On the other hand, I can't think of an American artist who would deal with your subjects in precisely the same way—with your irony in the past, and with your uninhibited gaiety in the present. Even pop art and the new realism are burdened by more self-righteous attitudes. Artists take themselves too seriously, and there is a dearth of wit in their works.

WC: When I was painting in Paris (for thirteen years) I was an American in Paris. I was a tourist. Certainly, I could not have avoided being influenced subconsciously by European standards and aesthetics. There is no such thing as an expatriate. An expatriate only goes to another country so he can live off the cheapness of their economy.

Actually, it took foreigners to make Americans aware of their own pop culture—Hamilton, Alloway, Paolozzi, and others. They began looking at American pop before Americans did: after all, they had been deprived of all the pop goodies by the war.

SH: One would think Paris might have turned you toward a more formal art.

WC: I was already a painter. The French didn't do me any harm. I was never very badly bitten by the École de Paris. I am a nut! I never became a Frenchman.

SH: Nevertheless, I am sure that surrealism in France and

individual surrealist artists have been important to you and helped you arrive at your present subject matter.

WC: I came back from the war looking for trouble. I tried to find it in politics, but I ended up on street corners giving out handbills; that wasn't much fun. I needed something to set me on fire—the war was a shock. People were shooting at me. Why was someone taking all this trouble to shoot at me . . . Most of the time they were Americans, once in a while Germans. After the war, the surrealists provided something unique: I developed a new philosophy based on new friendships. I had just finished reading James Joyce and to my mind he was the most revolutionary writer in terms of image and expression. I started to paint in the hopes that sharpening my visual perception might help sharpen my literary perception. I was also fortunate to receive encouragement from friends such as Man Ray, Max Ernst, Marcel Duchamp. I was very much a primitive—I never studied formally—and I will never forget what Marcel said to me, the greatest words of encouragement I ever received: "Why don't you go on painting."

SH: Did you ever feel suffocated by your close association with the surrealists?

WC: No. One of the things I brag about is that every time I go to my studio, it's as if I never held a paintbrush in my hand before.

SH: Can one be so innocent?

WC: Since I have never been aware of or have never taken seriously the concept of "masterpiece," painting is the only activity that keeps me from becoming more peculiar than I am.

SH: How did the surrealists' imagery of women affect you?

WC: I can never forget that the surrealists were victims of the same sort of Victorianism that I inherited. The romanticism of Surrealism is post-Victorian. It was repressive and romantic at the same time and had to be expressed in that ambivalent way.

SH: Your style has enlarged recently—both plastically and technically. You have made advances in these new figure compositions.

WC: I don't think there has been any progression whatsoever. One can go backward or forward, it doesn't really matter very much. There is no such thing as progress in art. You only change because you're bored with what you've done. You want to do something else. Duchamp, in all the years I knew him, never used the words "better than."

SH: Your general style certainly has not changed.

WC: There are things I did in old pictures that technically were a lot of fun, but I couldn't do them again. Actually, I have destroyed pictures I did not understand, but in looking bock, if I'd kept them, they'd be years ahead of what others have done lately.

SH: As Roland Penrose suggested, it's really impossible to place you in any "school." Some of Magritte's enigmas or Duchamp's puns seem related to what you are doing, and your fantasy reminds me of Ernst, but still you seem more a part of our own time. On the other hand, you are not obsessed with pop or commercial culture. If you could be considered a Prophet of Pop, it would be on a very personal basis.

WC: You don't move life, life moves around you. Life moves around you and plugs you into a position. It happened to Duchamp.

SH: Have you given much thought to reactions your show might provoke among women, particularly the Fem-Lib group?

WC: They will probably burn me in effigy and that will be their fault. The whole point of my subject matter is to express joy.

SH: I am sure you do not have an explicit program in mind for releasing or exorcising the demons of sexual repression in these works. Still, these paintings are fun. I also find an interesting tension between the erotic—no matter how caricatured the action and the decorative elements. The subject matter is absorbed into pattern and lively surface, and you end up looking a little like Matisse.

WC: I don't agree at all.

SH: The subject matter is . . . ?

WC: Erotic. I paint them like I would paint a landscape or a still life.

SH: I find it difficult to overlook the focus on genital regions, for example, and the coupling figures.

WC: Well, that's where we disagree. I find that oboes, or pianos or my French horns (in my last exhibition) get me quite aroused. These fornicators don't do much for me.

SH: Well, just how do you see them?

WC: They are essentially still lifes: they are flowers.

SH: About your visual sources: I understand many of the compositions come directly from photos in Times Square hard-core porno magazines, and I see your studio contains a sizeable collection of them.

WC: It's highway robbery. I went to Times Square—into one of those really crummy joints—and I said to the salesman, "Now you may think this is funny, but I'm an artist, and I'm looking for . . ." And the guy says, "Yeah, yeah, in the back room."

SH: Are they expensive?

WC: Very. But, every once in a while I find an image I simply can't resist.

SH: Have you invented any new techniques in these works?

WC: There's been too much history for any inventions to be left.

SH: Did you paint this show to be provocative or sensational?

WC: I painted it out of absolute necessity. These are paintings presented as paintings. The show simply had to be.

CPLY by Vincent Fremont

Originally published in *Interview*, February 1976

VINCENT FREMONT: I know you were adopted at a very early age by the Copley News Service Family. What was your childhood like?

BILL COPLEY: Well, my parents were a lot older than I was. It was a very dull and boring childhood in Illinois, then California.

VF: Did you become sort of the black sheep of the family very quickly?

BC: I managed that after the War.

VF: What about before.

BC: Before I was trying to conform, though not very successfully. I always got sent to these schools that I didn't want to go to. I didn't want to go to Andover for chrissakes! I didn't want to go to Yale for chrissakes!

VF: When you were a kid, was your family collecting art or books?

BC: My family was not particularly cultured. They had a lot of art and it was so bad it was unbelievable! It was the kind of art that you would collect if you didn't know what you were doing.

They had some American painters, some European. Everybody was nobody and half of them were fakes anyway. The kind of stuff you would buy in furniture stores. I often think that I was probably helped a lot by bad art. It was all around me so I had to protect myself from it. I had to get something out of that. Like one time I was with Duchamp at a restaurant downtown— Luchow's. It was when I was first knew Duchamp and I took him to Luchow's; I didn't know any better! It was in the summertime and he didn't have a coat on and we had to borrow one from the waiters.

VF: When was this?

BC: It must have been in 1947. Anyway there was a painting on the wall next to our table and I was trying to impress Duchamp. I said, "Isn't it a lousy painting." And in a very nice way he spent a half hour telling me what was good about it! I think that bad art is very inspiring.

VF: You became interested in Surrealism, became totally involved, why?

BC: I was looking for something, you see. The War had very definitely turned me into a left-winger. I got involved with the Henry Wallace movement, and all that kind of thing. It wasn't really satisfying, but Surrealism was. It was very satisfying. It filled that void. I was looking for something, I found it, and that was it. As a painter I have never been conscious of being a Surrealist—I think what I have to think. I don't know what controls that. I only call myself a Surrealist simply because of my association with the people themselves, and the fact I agree with those people, I am at home with them. Surrealism is so misunderstood in this country. Surrealism simply has to do with recognizing something that has always existed. Surrealism never invented anything, they recognized things that have always been there. Surrealists rediscovered African primitive art. The greatest collection of primitive art at the time was owned by Breton. Most artists here feel they have to put it down because it is competing with them in some strange way. So Surrealism is a dirty word in America. It doesn't have to be. It's not competing with anyone. It's an attitude, a way of looking at things.

VF: Did you exhibit any of your early, beginning works?

BC: I had a small show, my first, at Royer's Bookshop in Los Angeles. Royer had this bookshop and his wife was a painter; he sold mostly pornography. At that time I met Max Ernst, Man Ray . . .

VF: How did you meet them?

BC: Through my gallery. I started a Surrealist gallery.

VF: How did an unknown gallery get them?

BC: We were an unknown gallery but also they were unknown.

VF: You mean there wasn't anyone around that wanted to handle them?

BC: No. The artists were all broke.

VF: When was this? In the late 1940s?

BC: Yes, 1947 or 1948.

VF: There were no wealthy collectors in those days buying their art?

BC: No, none at all. An enormous Max Ernst would sell for a thousand dollars. A large Tanguy was selling for $750!

VF: Whose paintings did you exhibit at your gallery?

BC: We had Magritte, Tanguy, Cornell, Ernst, Matta, and Man Ray. We ourselves bought ten percent of every show. In other words we guaranteed that they would get at least ten percent of the show sold because there were no buyers. That is how I got my collection started.

VF: Did you ever buy more than just ten percent of the shows?

BC: In a couple of cases I did. I bought all of Cornell's work. I had fifty Cornells!

VF: Do you still have them?

BC: I have two left.

VF: What did you do with them?

BC: I gave them away to my friends. Cornell didn't speak to me for three years because I doubled the prices. He was trying to sell his work for $100 and I was going to sell them for $200!

VF: Are you collecting art anymore?

BC: I haven't been collecting lately, but I'm thinking about starting again. Just out of curiosity, I want to see if I still have an eye. I think I will start with kids again. I'm very interested in conceptual art. A lot of it isn't good but some of it is.

VF: You used to design your own chess sets. Was this because you were influenced by Surrealist artists that you knew?

BC: Yes, sure, they all made chess sets. Tanguy made a set, Max made a set, Duchamp, and Man Ray made a lot of sets. I made a wonderful set and my wife threw it out. It was made out of bottles. The rules that I set down were that they had to be bottles you can find in a liquor store, you couldn't alter them at all. It took me ten years to figure it out. I finally got it all together. There would be red wine in one set and white wine in the other. The idea being if you capture a piece you have to drink it. It's not my idea unfortunately, it was either Breton's or Julian Levy's. Julian Levy once designed a set based on cocktails, and if you capture a piece you had to drink it.

VF: Why were they designing chess sets?

BC: The Surrealists were very funny. The first ones were so devoted to Breton. E. L. T. Mesens was a very promising young musician. When he found out that Breton didn't like music, he stopped composing.

VF: Did he ever write music again?

BC: He never went back to music, he ended up making collages. Duchamp, I think, was the one that got them all making chess sets. He was very much into chess in the beginning. They all played chess because they felt they had to, they were that much of a club at that time. It didn't last very long, they started to get excommunicated one by one. Breton tried to be a dictator.

VF: After Breton kicked everyone out, who was left?

BC: Just himself and a couple of frumpy old painters, and a lot of disagreeable young poets!

VF: When did you go to Paris?

BC: Shortly after the gallery closed. My marriage broke up after the gallery or at the time of the gallery. I rented an abandoned firehouse in Los Angeles. I had chess evenings, stiff like [*sic*] evenings . . .

VF: Who were you seeing in LA those days?

BC: I was very close to Man Ray at the time.

VF: He was living in LA.

BC: Yes, he and I went to Paris together. He came to the firehouse one night and said, "I've had it with this town." I said that I'd had it too. We both went to Paris the next day.

VF: Why did you choose Paris?

BC: I got to meet the people I wanted to see. I met them before they died. I got to meet most of the Surrealists, and the Surrealists' entourage. The only one I didn't get to meet was Picabia, and I was sorry about that. He was an astounding personality. I lived in France for thirteen years. I finally got a house outside Paris.

VF: Can you talk about your painting?

BC: Well . . . I'm not whatsoever an abstractionist, it means nothing to me. My paintings are almost literary statements. This is why it originally tied in so well with Surrealism. I find Abstract Expressionism a horror. It's fine for those people who like it. I'm much more a literary person, as a painter . . . My paintings are a little like statements, like a poem is a statement.

VF: So you develop a single theme for your shows, like your new one, *1776 and All That*.

BC: Yes, a show is like a movie, it needs a title.

VF: How do you go about putting together images for one of your themes?

BC: My work can be based on an idea, a phrase, or a proverb. Some of these things are so crazy that they immediately inspire a visual comment. I had a lot of luck with the Sears Roebuck catalogues, they have wonderful images. Also they have a lot of nostalgia to help them along. Some of the things are the same today as they were then. In that series I had to concentrate on not thinking. I would go through catalogues as fast as I could and make selections. Then I would try not to react at all consciously and as fast as I could make a drawing from the image. I took the same thing and would make a painting from it as fast as possible. My reaction was sometimes nostalgic, sometimes sexual. I tried to make it as much free association as possible. I did an erotic show, which I sort of stumbled on. I went down to Times Square and bought myself armfuls of dirty magazines. There again I went through them quickly. When [one] would arrest my eye I would tear it out and put it aside until I had a large stack. After the show at the NY Cultural Center I didn't want to do it anymore—I didn't want to be known as a dirty painter anyway. Then I didn't know what to do next, I was going crazy. Then Brooks Jackson, from Iolas, came by and said, "Why don't you do a Bicentennial show?" I started right away.

Advice to a Young Artist

Anne Doran
Originally published in *CPLY 1919–1996: The Art of William Copley*
(Forum for Contemporary Art, St. Louis, 1999)

*I met Bill Copley in 1981. I had been out of art school for two years
and had just moved to New York. As he said in one of his first letters
to me . . . ten years from now or even next week what will it matter
if you were in this show or not? And twenty years later, I cannot, for
the life of me, remember what show it might have been or anything
of the studio visits or love affairs that prompted my anguished letters
to him. But I do remember his advice, and the generosity with which he
gave his love, his support, and his knowledge of art and the world.*

*For Bill, the worst crime was to be humorless, and not living fully was
a close runner-up. He was funny, outrageous, and honest, and he used
everything in his art. He once wrote to me, "Show me a work of art
that is not autobiographical and I'll show you virgin birth." Even now,
no matter how unhappy, ridiculous, or infuriating the situation, if I ask
myself what Bill would say about it, the answer comes back immediately.
Enjoy it. Acknowledge it. Make it count. Other people taught me how
to make art. CPLY taught me how to be an artist.*

—Anne Doran

August 8th, 1981
Roxbury

Annie:

Lesson number one. Or rather instruction of first importance to a relatively innocent young lady. No one, but no one has the right to do to an artist what that person did to you. Drop whatever you are doing, find that person, and if you're too timid to kill them, or afraid of going to jail (it would be preferable however to kill them as they probably do this kind of thing all over the place and getting away with it and will in the future), at the very least tell them to go fuck themselves at the top of your lungs. Theirs is criminal behavior.

Of course you have suspicions that you are wrong. Any artist has these feelings all of the time and will always have them. It's not for them to kindle.

There is enormous value in layering a few sheets of paper with multitudinous images in a compulsive manner. There is enormous value in making pee pee on them if it has to do with what you want to do.

I once had a plumber working in my place in Paris object to the blue I was using. I could never finish the painting. You go and put your faith right back into your muddling and mincing and don't neglect to kick that person in the groin.

The surrealists have a number one rule. Never submit a work to a juried show. This person is judging your drawing. Your drawing has committed no crime so why should it be judged.

Seriously, or even more seriously, ten years from now or even next week what will it matter if you were in this show or not?

To become an artist you must refuse to submit to this kind of mentality on all levels. It's funny—in a piece I just got through writing I made this statement: "There is nothing negative to be said about an artist's work that he has not thought of himself."

I am livid. My day is ruined. You have ruined my week. You will drive me to drink again. Promise me, oh promise me that you will never fall for this shit again. And I am serious in advising you to withdraw. At least demand a mistrial.

You become an artist not to be a success, but to take vows for a frightening, frustrating, painful life that others will not dare undertake.

So I got the plans off for the monument.
I've done the poster.
I've done the text for the catalog.
I have another text to do but with a more humane deadline.
I am able to paint again.

Miss you too.

CPLY

March 11, 1982
Western Union

Merde,

CPLY

March 12th, 1982
Key West

Anne:

Your letter caught me here in Key West. The most frightening
thought to think someone might have taken given advice. Can't
even take my own.

Seem to paint well down here. Feel relaxed and out of focus.
Paint things I usually don't. I don't demand I understand what
I do. Up north I feel New England morality and have a different
attitude. Try more to know what I am doing. Trouble is I can't
stop working even when I want to. Like the salt mine at the bottom
of the sea. Still hung up, I guess, on mental undressment. Paint
what comes out.

. . . I doubt too, if intelligence is all that necessary to make an
artist. Sensitivity is. Surprisingly, talent has very little to do with
it. There can be no stars or prodigies. Seeing as how humility is
a prerequisite too. It's "To light the dusty way . . ." Not everybody
understands this. More on this if I get to see you.

Love,

CPLY

June, 1983
Roxbury

Anne:

It seems that everything I plan to say becomes a platitude before I get it out. I discover this is why I can't write. I realize too that my sudden discovery that I've aged isn't that big a deal. I'm not the only one it's happened to—others have been here before.

Years ago I proposed two dictionaries: a dictionary of ridiculous images and a dictionary of platitudes. I intended to complete the first, at least to the point of providing a sufficient pool of such to pull them individually and randomly from a hat and then unravel the modus operandi of Hieronymus Bosch.

The dictionary of platitudes was planned to be open-ended.

Living is vast and all thought and experience is destined for the slag heap of platitudes.

So I've shrunk my head and now I know why I can't write. I can scribble away.
Look at this way.

"X" being the possibility of being right.
"Y" being the certainty of being wrong.
"Z" being that somebody said it a long time before.
"P" being a platitude.

Then:

$$\frac{X \text{ times } Y = P}{Z}$$

The dangers are:

"C" believing what you say yourself.
"D" having someone believe you.
"L" license to talk.
"A" art, of course.

$$\frac{X \text{ times } Y = P - (C + D) = L = A}{Z}$$

To be on the safe side I am providing a supply of salt grains to be applied to whatever I have to say.

Otherwise I love you.

CPLY

178

March 2nd, 1984

Annie:

Have your letter and sense your malaise. You probably don't want to admit to yourself yet that you have made an important step toward proper awareness.

Going back to old conversations: yes we are a monogamous animal, but safely so only as long as it involves open-ended and mutual choice. Nature insists that we mate and that we have mates. But in the civilized world we must explore loneliness till we know ourselves like the back of our hand before we consider taking a mate. Marriage kills monogamy because it purports to be a life sentence. Proper mates must choose each other and renew the choice every morning. This has nothing to do with love. What's good for General Motors is good for America, if you remember this quotation. We must love and forgive ourselves.

This is brought on by way of congratulations.

Thinking in images is another sign of advancement toward freedom. It's already beyond thinking in words and morals. It's also what surrealism is all about. The metaphor soars above the simile. A successful metaphor provokes catharsis. Only our dreams are the truth.

Enough for now. Chew on that while I go back to work.

Tell me more about the show.
Did you get the grant?
What are you working at?

As for me: Have confined myself to solitary. Somehow most necessary. Never done it properly before. Mostly thinking about my work and losing weight. I'm hoping that my parole will come out of my work. I'm tempted to call it the Egg and I. Oval formats, the automobile as an egg with its interior exposed. I don't understand the compulsion to speak through the car. The sexual implications are enormous. "Footprints on the dashboard upside down." "The Blue Chrysler."* The important thing is it has me fascinated.

For a hobby, I've been enlarging my bird collection. Beebe built me a huge cage while I was away. Decided I didn't want a pet, birds are more fun to look at, so now I have two cockatoos, one blue and gold, one red, and multicolored macaws and an African Gray parrot. Project is to get them all to talk dirty.

Go back for my second new eye in a couple of weeks. Weather has been largely good with intermittent cold spells. Hope for improvement. 7 new paintings 24 drawings so far.

Thus is the world according to CPLY.
Trying to overhaul my brain.
Miss you too.

*Ed Kienholz

Love,

CPLY

Letter to Judith Young-Mallin

Young-Mallin Archive
Philadelphia Museum of Art Library and Archives

Dear Judith,

About all I can do at this stage is to compliment you on the
quality of the material you have sent me.

In retrospect I regret somewhat that I fled the US as hastily
as I did after the demise of my gallery. Passing through New
York I felt a strong temptation to tarry and become part of what
was beginning to happen. By not doing so I became a part of
a generation senior to myself. These people changed and made
my life, but they've died off on me and left me very sketchy on
the American aspects of surrealism.

Abstract expressionism I always considered to be a willful
misunderstanding of what the surrealists had to offer the country.
The scene that resulted never had any interest for me. To a large
extent I fall between the cracks of what your book is all about.

An interesting aside for you might be the activity of the Maison
Lefebvre-Foinet and the two brothers René and Maurice.

The establishment manufactured high-quality oil paints.
The grandmother was famous for her frugality, but maintained
the tradition of supporting the struggling artist. One story about
her described how she used to work the paint off of canvases grate-
fully donated to her to make cloths to chase dust with. A number
of Douanier Rousseau's were said to have met this fate.

There were two sons, René and Maurice. Maurice was shy
and retiring, René was the charmer and seducer. It was their

habit to leave packages of paint tubes on the doorsteps of needy artists, Victor Brauner, Serge Charchoune, probably Tanguy, Max maybe, etc., etc.

I met René this way while he was visiting in Hollywood. In Paris the brothers were famous for spoon-feeding arriving American artists. René died in a car I lent him when I had to return to the US for my step-mother's funeral. His brother Maurice immediately took over the role of charmer and seducer. Ask Dorothea about them. René introduced me to the area where I presently reside, Roxbury, Connecticut. Through him I met Sandy Calder and the Tanguys. L'affaire Gorky took place in Roxbury. Julien Levy was just next-door in Bridgewater.

René first took me to visit Calder. His studio had been a barn. When he opened the big barn door the wind brought what seemed like hundreds of mobiles to life.

Calder induced us to visit the Tanguys which was something of a mistake. Sandy and Yves took one look at each other and started boozing. Kay was not happy with us.

Anyway consider me a cheering section and as the French say for good luck "merde."

Bill CPLY

A Conversation with William Copley by Alan Jones

Originally published in *CPLY: William N. Copley* (David Nolan Gallery, 1991)

The leaves were turning Rita Hayworth red across the improbable undulating hills of sexual Connecticut, legendary hideout for Surrealist masterminds Yves Tanguy and Hans Richter, as the car turned up the gravel lane at a sign marked CPLY. This was no maple syrup farm. My assignment: locate and question none other than Bill Copley, alias CPLY, America's greatest Surrealist painter. From French prison slang and the working method of Hieronymus Bosch to the restaurants of Montparnasse and Marilyn Monroe's dialogue, the investigation fell open like a suitcase of dirty laundry. This had to be the place . . .

—Alan Jones

I started off wanting to be a writer, but after reading James Joyce I concluded that the problem with my writing was its lack of imagery. So I decided to try painting, just to see if I could stimulate myself along those lines. But I started liking it too much and never went back. And I do know how to write, but I still don't know how to paint. Had I taken it seriously I don't think I would have had the freedom that I started with. I guess that's what saved my life. If you know what art *isn't*, the whole world is before you.

I was in California, just back from the War, when I first encountered Surrealism. My brother-in-law had studied painting and worked for Disney. He gave me a very complete course in Surrealism. It fascinated me from the beginning. Although I don't believe that I really paint quite like a Surrealist, I've always felt that I have a Surrealist *mentality*. You start with the quote from *Les Chants de Maldoror*, "The chance meeting of a sewing machine and an umbrella on a dissecting table." A Surrealist painting can be made at any time from three such elements. The subconscious mind is constantly forced to make associations. But while these associations exist anyway, since everything in nature has a relationship, you can actually improve on the process: that, I think, is Duchamp's great contribution. He pushed it further, so that you had more of a choice in the associations you were making.

I was very young when I opened my gallery in Los Angeles. It was 1948, and to me the Surrealists were gods descended straight from Mount Olympus. Max Ernst, René Magritte in particular, Yves Tanguy, Matta, Joseph Cornell, Man Ray—I was really worshipping them when I showed their work. The easiest thing to do is to knock at somebody's door and say, "You don't know me, but . . ." Surprisingly enough it works, which is wonderful. You don't get thrown out too often. And in my case, it changed my life. I'd been a pretty square character up to that point, and discovering the Surrealists was the biggest thing that had ever happened to me.

What impact did this exposure to Surrealism have on your own development as a painter?

It was an overwhelming discovery to see that this degree of freedom was even possible. Without formally studying art in any way, shape, or form, I suddenly found myself running a gallery, living day by day with these paintings around me. A painting does have the power to subvert, and they got to me, subconsciously. Paintings are meant to subvert, to release us from the constraints which society puts on our thinking.

The gallery was a total disaster. We sold three paintings the first day, and I thought we had it made. The guy who owned Coca-Cola came in blind drunk, made us get drunk with him,

and wrote out a check for three paintings. No one ever picked
them up. I never saw him again, and I never sold another painting.
We spent six months putting the gallery together, and had another
six months of shows. Then it folded. But while it lasted we
made sure to serve enough booze at our openings so everyone
came; movie stars appeared for the drinks and never came back.
A shortage of collectors was never the problem in Los Angeles.
The problem was that they went to New York to buy. There was
a kind of chic about bringing a painting back from New York.
I had a show of Joseph Cornell, and people would say, "Oh my
god, I thought this was an art gallery." Cornell didn't talk to me
for a year because I doubled his prices—from $100 to $200. Still
we didn't sell anything. I owned fifty of his works, then before
I went to Paris I gave them all away.

   Stravinsky's daughter-in-law was our secretary. She could hardly
speak English, and I had to type all her letters for her. But the
Los Angeles art world was totally hostile. They only went as far
as Picasso. It's a strange town anyway. Culturally, it was a desert.
And those enormous distances: you leave your house and the next
time you look at your watch five years have gone by.

   Man Ray was living in Los Angeles at the time, but his influence
on me had already been established long before I met him. Man
was very badly treated in Hollywood. Of course they invited him
to dinner to benefit from his prestige, but then they wouldn't let
him do anything. They wouldn't let him play. But he was endlessly
amused by Los Angeles. "Why do anything," he'd say, "when
there's so much more Surrealism in this town than I could ever
invent." But I think he always had his feelings hurt that he wasn't
recognized. He worried about that. And I always wondered why.
They got him to go out to Hollywood and then got cold feet and
were afraid to let him do anything.

   I hadn't been painting much during the time I had the gallery.
When the gallery closed I went over to Europe with Man. Then
I met the Surrealists, and ended up staying in Paris for thirteen

years. In one sense, going to Paris was probably one of the biggest
mistakes of my life. New York was in the process of reinventing
painting according to its own ideas. New York was where the
action was. Maybe I'd read too many Victorian novels—go to
Paris, live in a garret, and learn the hard way. But that too saved
my life. It kept me from taking art too seriously. The French take
art very seriously, and I just couldn't help wanting to bait them
a little. They were really so damn shockable.

What was happening in Paris when you arrived in the early fifties?

The Surrealists were still the vedettes. Man and I were
members of the same club: when you knew the Surrealists you
wouldn't know anybody else—or want to. It was a distinct
minority, and we propped each other up. Nowadays New York
artists seem afraid to talk to each other, and that's a bloody
shame. A lot of ideas just die as a result. Paris had two worlds:
respectable art on the Right Bank, and the Left Bank where
everyone met and talked. Artists were very supportive of each
other. They never felt they were in competition, but more
like co-conspirators.
   Not getting to know Picabia is the one thing I regret most
of all. He was quite ill, and I was afraid to bother him. I regret
it. He did so much wonderful writing—anti-writing, just as his
painting was anti-painting. You think of him, and of course you
have to think of Jarry. I missed the real fun by twenty years.
They were all pretty much over the hill by the time I got there.
But they must have been a real lively bunch in their day, because
they were still up to something all the time—that, I remember.
They liked sex and they did something about it. In the beginning
they had been beating the drum about making a real effort to
include women artists. Later they sort of got conservative again.
Their whole attitude was a first attempt at sexual liberation.
In the beginning the women went from hand to hand. It was in

the Surrealist style to trade them off. Dalí's wife had been with Éluard. Sometimes they went three or four times around. But it was funny to see them together, later, because as much as they would pretend they were doing whatever they felt, you could still feel the jealousy in the room. These are the real Olympians, those who made a clean break from common sense, to highly organized non-sense.

With writing as your point of departure, how did narrative methods function in your work as a painter?

Magritte answered that best. It has to do with assembling images. But certainly in a way not so much by chance, but with intent. And I mean, in the case of Magritte, the assembling of images accomplishes a tremendous expansion of awareness, by associations that open the mind to subtle relationships. For a long while I employed a sort of private mythology in my own work, like the cast of characters in a play. I rolled them out like dice. One thing I've always admired is Pre-Raphaelite painting. It is narrative, and you can fill in the gaps any way you want. There used to be a guard at the Tate who would catch you looking at the Pre-Raphaelites, and he'd jump out and start to explain them to you with the most hilarious theories.

My life is a quest for the ridiculous image. The visual pun is the golden nugget that we seek. Joseph Cornell's paperweight made from compressed paper; Man Ray's *Pain peint*—all his objects were visual puns. You are not asked, you are absolutely forced to make associations. Visual puns are mind-expanding, imagination-expanding. It's all about heightening awareness. The viewer immediately has associations with experiences he has had that are equally ridiculous. Magritte is all about that. It's a can't-miss kind of humor.

The commedia dell'arte is a universal form, using the same characters time and time again—a jumping-off place for almost anything. And the same thing always happens, as in *Petrouchka*. I had never paid much attention to commedia dell'arte, but when I did I realized that it was where I had been all the time. It appealed to me because it is a very limited drama. In my commedia, it is always about being "taken in adultery." The typical situation is the embracing couple: the man is saying, *"Maintenant,"* and she is saying, *"Pas ici."* I love Pirandello. He asks what is reality? It's never the same for two people. Today there are so many court proceedings where everyone is describing something different. That's reality. No two people see a painting the same way, and no one ever sees it the way the painter intended.

I tend to be very single-subject-minded: for me the single subject is like the simple gag in vaudeville. The forgotten poet Robert Service is right down my alley—"The Face on the Barroom Floor." I can go through his work page by page, underlining images that translate straight into drawings. A small child lamenting, "Mother, there is no more to eat / Why don't you go back on the street?" I can't resist a line like that. Service used to be very popular, and now nobody knows his work, which is all the better because it makes me seem very original.

The writer O. Henry is in the same area. He has the kind of humor I like, bumbling W. C. Fields humor. And the eroticism is also bumbling. I maintain that when it comes to sex, everyone is a bumbler. That's what makes sex so much fun: since nobody really understands it, the possibilities for originality are endless. Imagine if everybody knew what they were doing. That would be terrible.

What other subjects are there besides sex? Painting is just the next best thing. It's kind of the same anyway. Both the *Large Glass* and *Étant donnés* are Rube Goldberg copulating machines. The Unknown Whore is certainly as important as the Unknown Soldier: they've both been *had*. Everybody forgets that a prostitute is a woman before she is a prostitute. We have a way of putting people in categories and keeping them there. A soldier is a man before he puts on a uniform, and what is more ridiculous than the Unknown Soldier? Anyone who lets himself be killed in a war deserves a monument to his stupidity. It makes as much sense as dying in a car crash.

Lately I've changed my way of working by trying to depend much more on the subconscious. I start a painting and just leave it. I know there is bound to be some subconscious event, so I don't stand and worry what to do next. I walk away from it. This was a big step for me. It got me away from my own formulas. Duchamp emphasized the balance between yourself and random chance. He had demonstrated that in the *Large Glass* by using a toy cannon. He dipped matches in paint and fired them at the glass, aiming where he *wanted* the paint to go, but knowing that the toy gun was very inaccurate.

Line has always been an important element in your painting.

Yes, but I don't know how it comes about. I've never tried to draw. I don't know *how* to draw. Picabia serves as a good example: if he needs something, he'll get it. I'm not out to impress anybody with how I draw. That's where my new step was most complete. Getting the painting to paint itself is magical. It's not art in the sense of setting out to "make a work of art." Picabia gave himself total freedom. He would paint the way he needed to, for what he was trying to do. So he really had no style; he had all styles. I once wrote that if Duchamp was the tortoise, Picabia was the hare.

In drawing, I've always thought that Bellmer was astonishing. Tanguy did drawings, but they were no different from his paintings. Matta was probably more of a draftsman than a painter—in a sense, he had his commedia dell'arte too, only with a cast of creatures rather than of people. Dürer, oddly enough, appeals to me because of the way he used perspective. He used it the way something should be used, never ornamentally. But perhaps one of my all-time favorite draftsmen is Harriman, the cartoonist who drew Krazy Kat.

Did friends such as Man Ray ever share with you their wisdom concerning studio routine?

Man Ray taught me never to clean your windows, because dirty windows diffuse the light for you; and of course never to sweep, because that would raise dust and you don't want dust in the air. But I think he was justifying the fact that he was too lazy to care. Somebody once asked Max Ernst his advice to fledgling artists, and he replied, "Tell them to cut off their ear." My advice is, whenever you do something you should immediately try to do the exact opposite. I think you have to have roadblocks that you place intentionally in front of yourself, so you have to make the effort to get around them. It's not an easy thing to do. But I don't intellectualize it at all; I just set myself up with something I can work with. When you get into a painting, when you put your second color on, you've already set yourself up a trouble situation.

I'm much better off doing drawings on expensive paper, because I know that I'll never be able to bring myself to tear it up if something starts going wrong. I can afford paper, but everyone has their weak spots. Buying a new camera or a new wristwatch scares the hell out of me. I once forced myself to buy twelve cameras, just to try to get over it. With drawing, if I get in real trouble I know I'll still have to find a way out of it. If I'm making a nude and end up scribbling it out, I feel terrible. So I make it into a cowboy with a long whip! I can't bring myself to throw it in the wastebasket.

When you think of it, there's really nothing more hilarious than the so-called art scene. Selling a painting—or buying one, for that matter—is a Surrealist act in itself. What prevents paintings from being considered commodities is the very fact that the prices paid for them never make any sense at all. That's what I love about Mexico. Every Mexican Indian is an artist, and the motivation is not money. Art is a way of living your life, not a business. It's too bad when kids come to New York and think they're going to have some kind of "career" as an artist: they're missing out on that whole other side, forgetting that the function of the whole thing is to liberate—they're afraid to take that one step that will liberate them from the whole thing. And New York intimidates artists. They end up having no fun at all, and *that* is bound to affect the work. In a place like Soho, the revolutionary is completely contained; as long as he is part of the scene he's not going anywhere, he's not going to upset anything.

You have to get completely away from the things society imposes on you, to get down to satisfying your own curiosity. That's what was so great about Andy Warhol: he was driven only by curiosity. He was too busy to buy himself a yacht or a Mercedes. He had to know *everything*, he had to know everybody else's business. He was an artist for himself. And Andy worked very hard at satisfying his curiosity. He was a very inspiring artist in that respect; there was absolutely nothing he wouldn't try. Yes. He knew Duchamp well. Andy would go over to visit at Marcel's a lot of times. I was there on a couple of occasions when Andy dropped by. Andy got a lot from Marcel, and revered him as much as I did. And both were completely misunderstood. The media never really knew what to say about Duchamp, or about Warhol, and when they don't know what to say they get cute. Very few people *really* understood what they were up to.

Surrealism was more than a mere *art* movement. In fact Breton always preferred the poets over the painters. But it was much more. It was revolutionary—in the nastiest way conceivable. It was anarchistic. It put you way out on a limb and taught you how to cut the branch off behind you. Why does the artist feel obliged to con people into believing he's respectable? What is this pretense of respectability? We really *are* dangerous. Our motives really are bad. If people knew what was going on inside our heads, we'd all be put in jail. Being an artist is the closest thing to being a criminal that exists. Your bitch is with society; just think of all the nasty ideas you can get away with! And nobody reads them very carefully: they think it's *art*. You can't paint with the object of feeding yourself—if you do, it becomes something else, a career. Art is *anti*-career. It's an anti-social experience.

You had already become acquainted with Marcel Duchamp before moving to Paris.

I got to know him in New York. Man and I went there first, on our way to Paris, and I saw quite a bit of Marcel. Katherine Dreier was still alive, and he took me up to visit her in Milford, Connecticut. When I walked into her house and saw his painting *Tu m'* on the wall, it hit me like a ton of bricks. This one painting, which is now at Yale, probably influenced me more than any other. The title implies *tu m'emmerdes*. What I get out of *Tu m'* is that Duchamp is suggesting that the number of dimensions, planes of existence if you will, are infinite. He demonstrates this by using shadows, by using paint sample cards, a painted tear, a real safety pin—all associations of a cosmic sort, made to show that this goes on forever. Duchamp carried painting a little further into metaphysics. That painting changed the course of my life. I've always been completely indifferent to painting-as-painting. I'm not impressed.

How did Duchamp react to your work?

All he told me was, "You should continue painting." He never talked much about his own work, he preferred to talk about other things. You had the feeling when you first met him that you'd known him all your life. He was so easygoing, you were not afraid to just talk. I had two great ambitions: one was to take Marcel to a baseball game; the other was to take him to Las Vegas. I thought baseball would fascinate him because of the mix of skill and chance, but he had the game all figured out before the first half. In Las Vegas, he got to play his system—the one he invented that wasn't intended to win at roulette but only to break even. He had Walter Hopps carry the chips. Marcel would just tell him which numbers to put them on. They played all night long—and broke even.

How do you explain Duchamp's secrecy, the outward appearance of almost total idleness behind which his last work was assembled?

He understood what a personal thing it was. Claiming he was no longer painting allowed him to buy time. Just as art doesn't exist, neither does time. If there is one virtue I would like to corner the market on, it would be patience. That's something an artist needs a lot of. Patience relieves you of all pressure, the pressure to *do*. Marcel already had the reputation; if he had let it be known he was still working everyone would have been trying to find out what he was up to. But nobody had any interest in what he was doing because nobody, including myself, knew he was doing *anything*. This gave him all the freedom in the world, for something like twenty years. If he had had his way, Duchamp would have let art out of Pandora's box. He freed it, therefore he is for the moment rather unknown. I mean, collectors will pay to own anything he handled, but few make any attempt to really understand him. He remains too subversive. And he never let himself get cornered, witness the urinal. Marcel had the kind of curiosity that is personally motivated, in and unto itself: *I want to find out what this universe is all about because I'm going to be part of it pretty soon.* That's way ahead of religion.

You were instrumental in bringing Étant donnés *to its home in the Philadelphia Museum of Art. How did you come to be among the first to learn of its existence?*

One day he called me up and asked me to come to his studio downtown. I went, and when I came in—I was speechless. Here was a complete work of such complexity, which no one imagined even existed. But there it was. Since the Walter Arensberg collection was already in Philadelphia, he wanted *Étant donnés* to go there also. The next time I went back to his studio, the work had been crated. Marcel said nothing. I think he knew that he was ready to die, that this was his last statement. Shortly after that he went back to Paris and we never saw him again.

As you continue to paint, what do you see as the living influence of Surrealism?

They opened doors. And once those doors are open, they're not easily closed again. They made things possible for each other. I think what they established was, let's face it: there is no such thing as art.

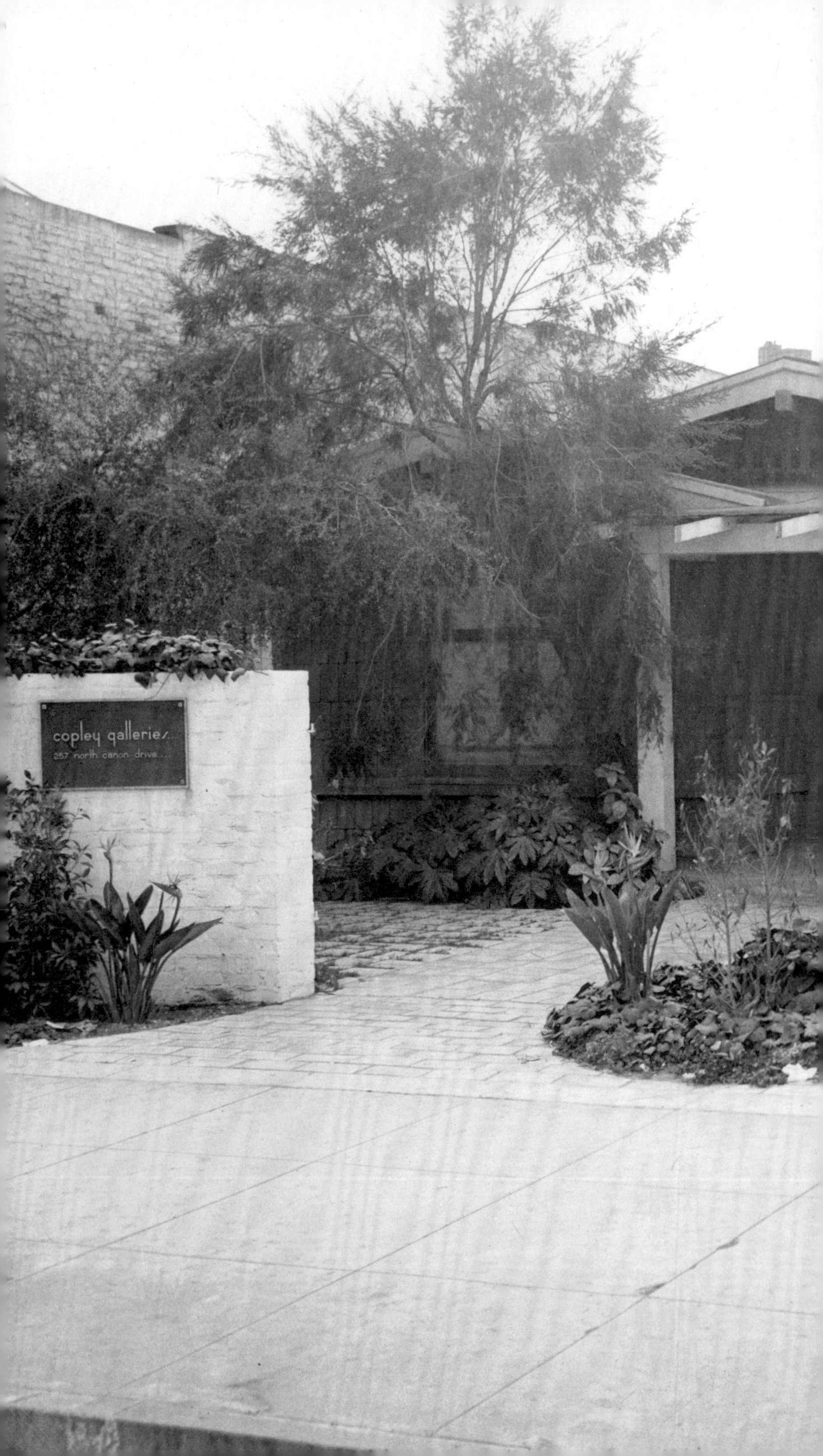
copley galleries
257 north canon drive

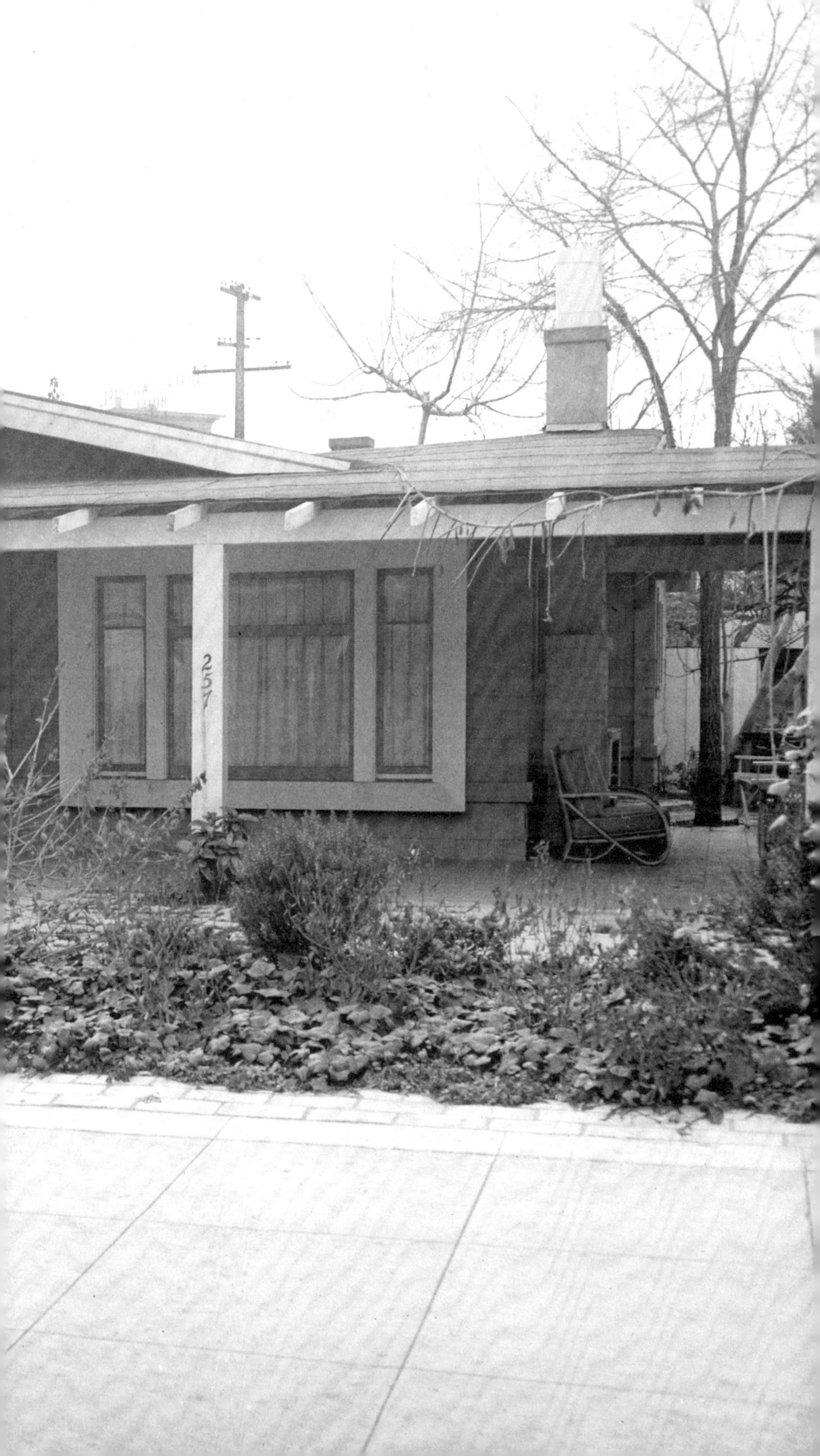

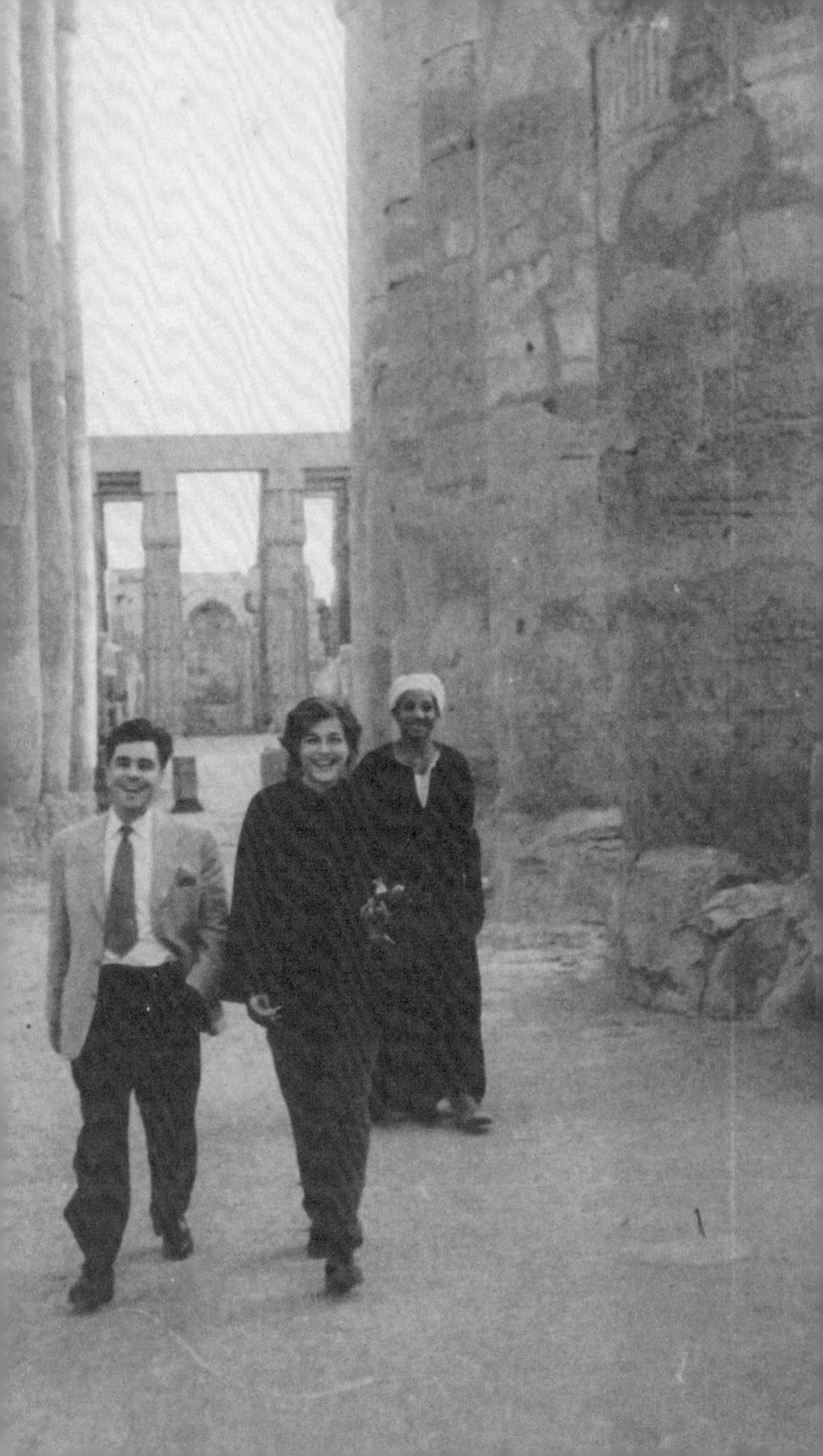

III. Early Writings

Copley Galleries to Show Works of Joseph Cornell

Originally published in *San Diego Union*, Sunday, September 26, 1948

An exhibition of the works of Joseph Cornell, brilliant American constructivist, will open at the Copley Galleries, 257 North Canon Dr., Beverly Hills, Tuesday.

Actual objects are used by Cornell to construct art forms which for the most part are reminders of childhood. For instance, one is a round, covered box, about 4 inches high and 8 inches in diameter. In its sides are peepholes for viewing the interior which is fitted with silver thimbles set loosely on straight pins. The box door is painted green, and the sides circled with many tiny mirrors.

The peeper almost surely jiggles the box enough to set the thimbles gently moving, and the effect is as enchanting as an Alice-in-Wonderland landscape. It seems that a myriad of miniature merry-go-rounds or perhaps parasols are whirling on multiplied greenswards—Cornell's subtle and irresistible invitation to recollect childhood.

Small glass bottles filled with varicolored sands set in rows in a teakwood showcase, prove a charming invitation to "revisit" the apothecary's shop. Other of Cornell's art constructions make a spectator nostalgic for some lost romantic moment of free happiness.

Cornell, who was born in New York City in 1904, had no formal training in art, and it was not until he saw the works of Max Ernst that he was inspired to create his unique personal poetry.

Picasso

Originally published as "Has Time to Be Human: Far-Famed
Artist Greets Travelers," *San Diego Union*, Sunday, July 1, 1951

PARIS, France—It is impossible to believe that he is seventy.
He is solid, not too tall, a little round. The little hair that's left
is white and bristly, but the sculpture of his head is harsh, and
you don't think of it as a sign of age. Everything about him
seemed brown, his skin through long familiarity with the sun,
the sweatshirt and the corduroy trousers through choice, and
his deep brown eyes that fix you like the darts bullfighters use.
He is a regular fan at the bullfights in the old Roman arena
in Nimes, in fact he had just returned from there the day I
met him.

We met the children first as they came running down the
path ahead of him. The boy was about four and greeted us enthu-
siastically with a splendid vocabulary of rather naughty words in
French and Spanish that his father pretended not to have taught
him, while the young mother stood by with an expression of
patience more than amusement. The little girl was two. Both
resembled their father only in the expression of the eyes, but
there it was unmistakable.

There was a dog, too, a huge but gentle boxer who resembled his master, as always seems to be the case with dogs.

We sat outside near the little cottage, underneath a tree
overlooking the town and green valley with its farms and vine-
yards. It was a problem to get anywhere at conversation with a
boy and a boxer wrestling for a place on your lap and a little girl
resorting to tears occasionally to try to her share of the fun.

Sooner or later we were going to ask him to show us his work but he anticipated our request. We drove to the studio, which was actually a farmhouse. In the first room, an enormous one, we saw sculpture. He had been working on the life-size figure of a mother goat in the middle of the room. It was still a little more than a skeleton, but we could feel the poetry and the humor.

There were two large rooms of paintings and one of them seemed to be his inner sanctum, where we saw the most recent things, more than a dozen large canvases devoted almost entirely to the subject of his children. Each painting seemed to breathe his love for them. These he showed us with no comment.

The other rooms were full of pottery. The floors were crowded and the walls were lined with shelves that buckled with the weight they supported. It was staggering to think that one man had produced this much. There was as much variety as there was output. It was obvious that this was the work he loved and he showed it to us piece by piece with a pride that was equal to the awe we felt. The quality was such that it would have been an insincerity had he restrained himself from admiring his work with us, and I felt that it was the strongest proof of modesty that he could not contain the enthusiasm he himself felt.

When we came to the largest, most important pieces, he had us sit outside while he brought them out one by one and set them on a wall before us. Mostly they were pots and vases in the form of human heads and strange animals, and as he brought out more and more and set them there upon the wall, we suddenly felt there must be bodies to them, as though these heads belonged to strange beings standing just beyond the wall watching us with a curiosity even stronger than our own. One of us remarked on this, and the artist agreed triumphantly.

And then he took us into the town of Vallauris to see still more of his pottery at one of the factories where he had his own work fired. The people in the town of Vallauris seemed to have no problem with this extremely controversial man. He was their friend and they were his. The dignity and prosperity of the town has increased incredibly since he came to live there and they are very proud of him. Also, they have very concrete tokens of his generosity. And there is the generosity that I noticed, the generosity of the man himself.

He took us on the way to see the work of one of the villagers, not because the work was extraordinary but because he knew what it would mean to her if he brought people to see her work.

I am thinking of the generosity of a man who has the wealth and recognition of the world and gives his time and courtesy to his guests and to his neighbors. For such a man I think the greatest generosity must be with time, for remembering that ocean of production I saw, I had to wonder how he was able to spend the time of day casually with anyone.

For me it is merely one of the wonders of the world. For Picasso, with all his responsibilities, with all his interest and participation in politics, has the time to be the most prolific artist of his day, and the time to be a human being.

French Newspapers

Originally published as "American in Paris: Reading Newspapers
Chore for Tourists in France," *Daily News-Post* (Monrovia, CA),
Thursday, August 30, 1951

PARIS—Lately I have been reading the French newspapers. It's a
chore; there are so many of them. Also, it's not like in America,
where you can drink your news with your morning coffee, or
just come home to it at night. In the first place, you have to go
out and buy your paper. They are sold in little stands at strategic
corners, usually by a woman somewhere over forty who invariably is absorbed in conversation with another woman somewhere
over forty.

Although the two may have been on the very point of breaking
it up, they add postscripts while you wait. You get unmistakable
glances suggesting, "Why don't you go away?" You wait while the
visitor starts to leave three or four times and returns each time
for a last word.

Then it's a tradition for the lady to putter with a stack of
magazines that might have been in danger of falling, although
you doubt it.

Suddenly she gives you her complete attention, rather defiantly,
you feel. And while you have been standing there with your money
in hand, you suddenly realize you haven't decided what paper you
want, and there are a dozen choices.

Each paper mirrors the point of view of one of the political
parties, and there are more parties than you can shake a stick at.

Le Monde has a good reputation. It's a little intellectual and
somewhat right of center. But even the liberals respect it because
it has some very significant writing.

There is a very good Paris edition of the *New York Herald Tribune* which gives most of the American and world news, but I can't stand the look the lady gives me when I ask for it. So, to find out what's going on, I have to buy half a dozen papers.

But there are so many wonderful things to do in Paris that unless it's raining I don't stay home all day and read the papers. If the weather wasn't so bad this year, I'm sure I wouldn't know what was going on at all. As it is, my life is a series of recurring shocks wherein, from time to time, I am brought back to the realization that the world seems to be going to pot instead of getting inured to it.

The Tour de France has provided relief lately. The Tour is about as important here as the World Series in the United States. So, while the Tour was on the papers were full of nothing else—and I didn't have so much of a reading problem.

The Tour de France is a bicycle race that goes all over France and lasts about a month. I perhaps became interested in it because of the names of two entrants, Koblet and Coppi. Both of these names sound exactly like what I have to give as my own name when I pass the concierge's door every night. My name means nothing to the French if I try to say it any other way.

Anyhow, Hugo Koblet won the Tour this year with a brilliant and aggressive style, and Fausto Coppi, who was the favorite of everybody, ate a bad artichoke before reaching Marseille or he might have won it.

The tour is about three thousand miles long and is done in twenty-four stages. They had an awful time getting over the Pyrenees because of the bad weather. Coming down someone fell off one of the mountains. Most of the riders complained that it was too rough this year and want shorter stages and more rest.

Koblet made about $25,000 out of it in prizes and in contracts to indorse handlebars and such, and there were pictures in the papers of his mother putting him to bed. He claimed that the hardest day was when it was over; everybody wanted to buy him a drink and get his autograph.

Since the Tour there has been some more rainy weather, so I am still keeping up on my reading. Needless to say, all the options confuse me, but it's worth the trouble. Someone is attacked in one paper and the attack is answered in another. It's like watching a free-for-all fight.

British Broadcasting Corp.

Originally published as "English Too Good: Near-Miss Scored with Radio Debut," *Evening Tribune* (San Diego, CA), Wednesday, April 23, 1952

PARIS—I really feel I must recount the story of my venture into the airwaves with the British Broadcasting Corp. It all came through my great fondness for the Coupole, one of my favorite cafés in Montparnasse, and through a set of circumstances over which I had no control. The Coupole is the kind of a place you'd love to be found in if some friends or relatives surprised you with a visit to Paris. I don't know how many short stories begin with, "I was sitting in the Coupole over a Pernod when . . ." It would be like being found on the terrace of the Shephards' Hotel in Cairo over a scotch and soda before the trouble. The reason for this is that the atmosphere of the Coupole goes with good lazy living, and if you want to be known as a gourmet you must make it a point to pose there several hours each day. After you've been there for a while Monsieur Freux, the proprietor, comes by and shakes hands with you. He is a short, jolly man, rather bald, impeccably dressed, and extremely proud of his establishment.

He is also a walking example of what you can hope to look like in later years if you eat regularly at the Coupole. His waistline represents that delicate balance, so highly respected in France, between the gourmet and gourmand.

So I was sitting in the Coupole over a Pernod with my good friend Jean Cortot when Monsieur Freux came by. Jean Cortot is the son of the famous pianist but he is also very much of a painter in his own right. As a matter of fact, he is one of the painters chosen by Monsieur Freux himself to do the new mural decorations in the Coupole.

Monsieur Freux is very loyal to the painters in Montparnasse and periodically commissions these murals to keep the place up to date with modern local trends.

Monsieur Freux was quite excited seeing Jean Cortot and sat down at the table with us. When Monsieur Freux sits down at the table with you it means you are going to get a drink on the house.

He was glad to see Jean Cortot because, as he explained, the British Broadcasting Corp. had told him they were coming around to do a reportage of the Coupole and he needed someone who spoke good English to help him out.

Jean Cortot, who speaks better English than I do, turned on me with a hungry grin and assured Monsieur Freux I was just the man he was looking for.

I started looking for the exit, there was no way out and, since I was fond of the Coupole and Monsieur Freux, and since I'd just had a drink on the house, I agreed to help out in any way I could.

The broadcast was to take place in the late evening and he asked us to come around just before dinner. Since this seemed to suggest the meal would be on the house, we agreed to invite all the hungry artists we knew and to see if we couldn't arrange a bang-up broadcast for Mr. Freux.

I arrived on time and it didn't look as if anyone else were going to show up. To make matters worse Monsieur Freux came by with a four-page manuscript, all in French, covering the history of Coupole. If you get stuck, he said, you can read this.

It certainly looked as if I were going to get stuck, and I had the image of Cortot and all our hungry artist friends safely at home and glued to their radios.

During the meal, which I had been planning to enjoy, I worked feverishly at translating Monsieur Freux's manuscript. A sinking feeling in my stomach ruined my appetite.

Then at the eleventh hour Cortot and the hungry artists marched in and had themselves a banquet. The crew from the British Broadcasting Corp. arrived with a tape recorder and interviewed the hungry artists, while I lurked eagerly in the background with my brilliant translation of Monsieur Freux's manuscript.

Finally I was told they had no use for me. They only wanted people who spoke English badly.

I told them to call on me if they ever wanted someone who spoke French badly and went off in a corner to sulk.

Now I am left with my translation of the history of Coupole which nobody wants.

Brancusi

Originally published as "Close to Fame: Brancusi Buddy
of Writer—Almost," *Glendale New Press*, May 1952

Paris—One of the things I like to include in my letters to my
artist friends at home is the announcement that I now am living
next door to Constantin Brancusi. If I say it the right way I can
give the impression that we are great buddies. I can even say that
it is thanks to Brancusi that I am able to keep my studio, and it's
not my fault if they assume we are chums. I only do this in hopes
they will turn green with envy, for the name of Brancusi is one
of the most venerated in the world of modern sculpture.

What I haven't told my friends yet is that, when I was finally
introduced to Brancusi and told him I was his neighbor, he flatly
denied it. Still, he must know I'm here because I've caught him
peeking at me through his door. And it's true that it's thanks to
Brancusi that I have my studio, and this goes for all of us who
inhabit the Impasse Ronsin, and we like to think that it couldn't
happen anywhere else in the world but in Paris. Brancusi appears
to be the oldest and perhaps the most beautiful man in the world.
I don't think anyone knows how long he's had his studio here in
the Impasse.

The Impasse has remained a quiet country-like spot while a
busy commercial district grew up around it.

About fifteen years ago the land was all bought up by the
Assistance Publique, which is the public ambulance corps of
Paris. At that time Brancusi was around seventy years old and his
huge studio had already become a forest of immense and
wonderful sculptures.

His studio and the dozen-odd studios surrounding were condemned at that time to be torn down to make room for a garage for the ambulances. By a special act of the French Government, this work has been postponed for the duration of Brancusi's lifetime. He must be eighty-five by now, but a look at him is reassuring to us and we're sure we're safe for another fifteen years.

But his presence is something more than a reassurance to the artists here; it's a solid inspiration. It makes us think that it may be worthwhile painting pictures or sculpting stones after all.

And it's not just that so much fame has come his way, because Brancusi himself hasn't been very impressed by that. Nor can we start to guess what use he has for money he gets from the sale of his sculptures, for they are sold at fabulous prices. He lives alone and he lives simply, as simply as he must have lived when he first moved here, before most of us were born, and it helps us to know that a lifetime of honest, patient work can bring this much peace and security, if nothing else.

He keeps to himself but will receive you graciously if you take the courtesy to phone him and ask to come. This rule applies to his closest neighbors and friends.

Once inside his studio, you can only be overwhelmed by the quantity, the size, and the beauty of his work, and as you're wandering around in a speechless state, you munch on little hard, red candies which the artist requires you to take from time to time. When he opens the door and swings it slightly, you know that it's time to leave.

Now that spring is here Brancusi is more beautiful than ever, for he wears a white workman's suit and a white skullcap which accentuate the sculpture of his face, with its soft eyes and abundance of silver-grey beard.

Each evening he starts off with his little string basket to do the little shopping that is needed for his supper, and no one knows or suspects that this is a famous sculptor.

Leaving Paris

Originally published as "Copley Goes Touring: Discovers France Outside of Paris," *Daily Bank Review*, June 1952

Cap D'Antibes—Getting away from Paris turned out to be considerably more of a stunt than I figured. In the first place, it cost me all the progress I'd made in the last two months toward getting on the right side of my neighbor, Monsieur Brancusi. We had just reached the point where we were smiling at each other when we passed. Now I'll have to start all over again.

He had been watching me for more than an hour while I was trying to get everything I owned into the car. I noticed that he was frowning. Finally he asked me where I thought I was going. I told him I was going to Antibes. "Young man," he said, with real disdain, "there is no finer place in the world than Paris." And with that he turned his back and again began pretending that I didn't live next to him. When my friends found out I was leaving, they all decided to go with me, or they decided to send their friends with me. This would have been all right if I had bought a bus instead of an auto. As it is, half of them are mad at me and the other half have decided to come visit me.

Everyone talks about leaving for the seashore this time of year. But it requires a certain effort actually to do it. When one of us finally gets around to it, it makes up everyone else's mind at the same time.

One way to get away is just to leave and say nothing. I tried this once and no one would speak to me for a week after I got back. I'm still trying to figure out what basic law I transgressed.

I get so fond of Paris that it's always a surprise to me to rediscover that everywhere else in France is lovely, too. It's wonderful to leave around five or six in the morning. You're in the country almost immediately. The roads of France must be the most beautiful in the world.

Wherever you go they're lined with trees and this time of year it's a green tunnel all the way. They just don't think of building a road without planting the trees, too, and it's all one operation to maintain the roads and prune the trees.

The land gets richer the farther south you go; the people get more independent, and the wines get better. A lot of these wines lose their taste the minute you try to transport them, they have to be enjoyed on the spot.

Every town in France, no matter how small, has something unique about it that is apt to make it world famous. It may be a cathedral or some Roman ruins or some caves or the wine or an industry that's original or just plain better than anywhere else.

This makes things tough on the tourist. If he really wants to see France he finally discovers that it can't be done. A normal lifetime just doesn't give him the time to get started. If he stops everywhere he really ought to he'll never get anywhere. If he doesn't stop he leaves a regret in every town.

So the best thing to do is to get calloused and stop only when you are hungry, tired, or thirsty. Even so, you don't get anywhere fast. You're expected to enjoy things; you're expected to savor a meal at least two hours, a drink at least half an hour. If you don't, they'll let you know sooner that they think you're an American.

This doesn't mean that they're angry, because they insist in liking us. But pity is worse than disdain.

And they like tourists. They get them from all over the world and they provide themselves with a lot of their own. As I said a long time ago, a tourist is the only one who will call another person a tourist.

Actually a large part of the French population make their living out of providing comfort, entertainment, and good food to people who are traveling. Almost all of them have their hearts in it and enjoy it.

Crime Passionnel

Originally published as "Good Show: Murder Trial in France
Proves Entertaining Affair," *Illinois State Journal*, Monday,
December 15, 1952

PARIS—The only thing that the French have that can compare at
all with an American presidential election is a crime passionnel.
The timing of the trial of Mme Yvonne Chevalier, directly on
the heels of our election, might have been prompted by a desire
not to be outdone. The show was almost as good and it's a shame
that it wasn't televised. It would certainly have been as entertaining as the Nixon affair which the French themselves consider
a masterpiece of showmanship.

We have long admired the quality of gallantry toward the
weaker sex and if it wasn't invented by the French, who will deny
that it is they who have carried it to the peak of finesse? When
Madame Chevalier emptied her revolver into her ambitious young
husband, minister, deputy, and mayor of the town of Orléans,
it was hailed as a crime passionnel and we all knew what was
coming. The trial was even moved from Orléans to Rheims to
avoid any expression of partiality for the husband. The audience,
almost entirely women, packed the courtroom and overflowed
into the street outside. From the moment that the trial started
one could be certain that chivalry was not dead. The judge was
particularly sympathetic and instead of the usual "accused stand
up" it was "Madame, will you please stand up."

Sitting a few feet from Madame Chevalier was Madame
Jeanne Pierraud, the femme fatale in the case, younger, prettier,
and much better dressed than the defendant. Beside her was her
husband whom the judge singled out for some embarrassing

questioning. "Don't you feel that if you had been more firm with your wife, Madame Chevalier would not be in this court?"

Monsieur Pierraud admitted that this was probably true but said that he had liked Monsieur Pierre Chevalier infinitely better than an acquaintance his wife had made previously. As a matter of fact he had found Monsieur Chevalier rather "sympathique."

In all fairness the judge did give Madame Chevalier to understand that she had transgressed. "You should have dominated this passion," he told her, and "I understand the calvary of your conjugal life, but for all that you had no right to dispose of your husband the way you did."

He then turned his attention to Madame la femme fatale and demanded why she had not broken off with the deceased. "I had no desire to," she replied.

"You have three children. Did you ever feel any shame?" the lawyer or the defense then asked. To which she replied, "Never." When the defense lawyer suggested that she was the one who should be in the prisoner's stand, the public rose and cheered, and the judge had to threaten to clear the court.

At this point the prosecutor said he had a certificate saying that one of Madame Pierraud's children was ill and required her mother's presence. "Let her go," the prosecutor said. "Let her go to her child and let her stay there." In summing up, the prosecutor addressed the court as though he were prosecuting the deceased and Madame Pierraud, though he did ask for a few months' imprisonment for the defendant, "to convince herself that she had paid her debt to society." The jury however, considered that the eighteen months Madame Chevalier had already spent in prison was quite sufficient, and an hour later she left the court a free woman amid a tumultuous ovation.

Now I ask you, what could be more charming? The French are wonderful. Tonight I am having dinner with an English girl.

Billy Beck

Originally published as "GI Gets New Identity," *Elgin (Illinois) Daily Courier-News*, Thursday, February 26, 1953

PARIS—For many veterans who sacrificed their formative years to the opportunity of winning the war, coming to Europe under the GI Bill offered more than just a chance for further schooling. Quite simply, they sought a new identity. The extreme of this was found in Spain, where the GI could enroll in courses on the noble art of bullfighting. I even toyed with the idea myself, as this is an identity I have always wanted to assume. But something would have to be done about the bulls.

The most charming story of this kind is about the GI clown of Montparnasse, whom the French insist on calling Billy Beck. His real name is Frank Billerbeck, and he came to Paris originally to study painting, only giving it up gradually to continue his career as a clown. He had always had that in the back of his mind, but he never had been able to do much about being a clown until he came to Paris. He had tried his hand at it in his Boy Scout group and at church dinners and such. But his father had died when he was fifteen, and he had been left with the responsibility of supporting his mother and his sister. During the war he was busy fighting.

Things looked lean and, as the expiration of his GI grant approached, he began to look at the café terrace entertainers with a new interest. These are the people who play you trumpet solos, or make lace out of tablecloths or pretend to do legerdemain, so they can't be accused of being beggars when the hat is passed.

Frank liked Paris and didn't feel like going home. So he sent for his clown costume.

At his first performance he was showered with coins before he even had a chance to pass the hat. When he bowed and walked away without gathering a single "sou" his reputation was made.

"On fait pas ca ici," meaning it had never been done before in France.

The simplest thing to do was arrest him, and they dug up an old law which made it wrong to appear publicly in costume except on holidays. He was made to perform at the station house to determine what right he had to consider himself a clown. Les Messieurs les Agents were impressed.

Billy Beck was fast becoming hailed as a mysterious clown of Montparnasse even though he wasn't becoming wealthy, since his triumph depended on his turning his back to a rain of silver.

In January 1951 a publicity agent for the oldest and best-known circus in Paris, the Medrano, arranged an audition for Billy Beck. Nobody laughed enough, and nobody saw him slinking back to Montparnasse. The agent had to find him to tell him he was hired.

Five months later he was offered a three-year contract by Medrano, but had to fight the opposition of three clown unions. At last one of these agreed to accept him as apprentice, and he now has his card.

All of which does not upset Billy Beck in the least. His troubles are over and his career begun. He's perfectly willing to consider himself an apprentice, and I've never met anyone more serious about his work.

It's always disconcerting to meet Billy Beck. I suppose it's because one always expects to roll on the floor with laughter when one meets a clown. In everyday life, he looks like someone who is serious about theology or atomic energy.

His performances are studies of the beautiful balance between dignity and the ridiculous which is reflected in the behavior of all we timid souls who wish to be aggressive when we mustn't be.

As his confidence has grown, he has relied less and less on makeup. His last gesture was to discard a putty nose, leaving him naked with his own.

Frank Billerbeck has found a new identity in Billy Beck. He has become a clown.

Antiquities

Originally published as "Ancient Tombs Numerous: Egypt
Antiquities Need Much Study," *Herald-News* (Joliet, Illinois),
Tuesday, April 6, 1954

CAIRO—Although we think that people are the nicest thing
Egypt has to offer, we think that something should be said about
the antiquities. We really can't tell one Rameses from another
and have to admit we didn't study it very much. We like to look
at things and the problem as we see it is how in the world does one
see an Obelisk if one is looking down into a guidebook instead
of up at an Obelisk. We wasted a whole day trying to settle this
point by following a group of tourists around the Temple of
Karnak. The only ones who looked up from their guidebooks at
all had cameras. They spent all their time turning the dials on
light meters.

We had intended to take a lot of pictures ourselves and would
probably still be at it except for an unfortunate accident that
occurred the first time we went to pick up our prints. We were
complimenting ourselves on pictures taken by an oil man from
Oklahoma who didn't know that he was admiring ours. It would
have been just as well if the man in the photo shop had said
nothing. When we got our prints back, we didn't like them at
all and stopped taking pictures altogether as did the oil man
from Oklahoma.

It is most frustrating to come to Egypt without learning how
nice the people are and merely intent on seeing the antiquities.
There are just too many of them.

The best way to go to this country is on a honeymoon since
one doesn't have to be frantic about antiquities and can afford

to let a few of them go by. There is a great deal involved in getting to an antiquity in the first place unless it happens to have been built next to a modern hotel. Most of them, however, are accessible either by donkey or by car. We would hesitate to recommend one over the other. A car may be more comfortable but an Arab is better equipped to drive a donkey.

Even with the guidebook one has to see an antiquity in order to know if he will like it. If you don't look at a long donkey ride as fun in itself you may be taking a chance. We always feel secretly obliged to start across the desert whenever a tomb is available. Some tombs are nice enough to want to stay in, particularly the ones with electricity already installed and a lot of bright paintings on the wall. Then there are those which can be lighted by the sun with mirrors.

But it was disappointing to travel half a day in wind and rain to find a tomb that is dark inside. Even if it hadn't been dark the pictures were scratched out because the king's successor was mad at him. All that's left is somebody's initials from Denver, Colorado. Fortunately we'd be been followed by about thirty Arab children who were just as pretty to look at as the nicest murals would have been, and much livelier company.

We only had to look at the Egyptian landscape to start to understand the art we were to see. For the most part the land is so incredibly flat that the space around any object makes the background pictorially nonexistent. This, we feel, is why the ancient artists were content to concern themselves with two dimensions only. Whenever it was absolutely necessary to show depth they were never at a loss for a solution, and they were perhaps even more adept at significant distortions than our modern painters. There was a great deal in the murals done on the walls of tombs that would not have looked out of place in an art gallery today.

The architecture impressed us mostly only in the older and smaller temples. As for the bigger brassier temples, we thought they looked too much like movie houses. Also we figured that those old kings weren't any the less dead for all the trouble they put themselves to trying to impress us. We respect a lot more the little men who didn't sign their names to the statues and reliefs that adorn the walls. We think they must have been nicer people.

Yes, of course, we got sold a little old scarab or two. There is a saying here that an antique is as genuine as its owner believes it to be, and they do make nice cuff links.

We're not really sorry at all about the things we didn't see. It helps us think that someday we'd like to come back to this country and see some more. But if we've missed a pyramid or a temple or even a tomb to spend another day with such friends as Sayed Mlatum, Tolba Fadlallah, or Abraham, son of Naman, we'd act very much the same if we came back.

House in the Country

Published in unidentified newspaper as "What About Marcel?
House in Country Everyone's Dream," Friday, July 30, 1954

PARIS—Perhaps we're getting old, but instead of packing up for faraway places we're trying a new approach to summer this year. We're simply moving a few miles out in the country. This is supposed to be the dream of every Frenchman, though it's not considered good form unless one has reached retirement age. Up to that point one is supposed to merely pack up his car and join the river of traffic heading south. Frankly it's too much effort for us this year, which may be why we think we are approaching retirement age.

We like to think of ourselves as sort of demi-castors. A castor is generally a fireman or a policeman or a bus driver who spends all his time off building himself a house in the country, finishing the job just in time to have a place to retire after twenty-five years of service. The practice is encouraged and a castor generally can float a generous loan for materials.

Also, of course, one can buy a house *en viager* at a great reduction from a sweet old couple, giving them complete use of the property during their lifetime. If you've figured it properly they should both be dead by the time you're ready to retire, at which time you can sell to someone else *en viager*. It's a practicable setup even if it isn't very cheerful. Even though there are risks involved the odds are apt to be pretty much in your favor.

We did buy a property with four walls but from this point on we're fast becoming castors. In moving out, our predecessors were careful to pack up all the pipes and electrical conduits, along with everything else movable that they felt was rightfully theirs. Fortunately, the walls were a little too cumbersome and at the last minute they decided to leave them.

We wouldn't feel so much like castors if it weren't for a running feud we've been having with Louis Quinze. We've nothing against Louis Quinze personally and we do wish he'd leave us alone.

It seems our house is full of Louis Quinze. As a matter of fact, everyone insists that the house is Louis Quinze. There is Louis Quinze *boiserie* and Louis Quinze *tapiserie* and Louis Quinze *tulerie* and Louis Quinze *masonerie*.

Our original intention was simply to remove Louis Quinze and start from scratch. We might have been all right if we'd kept this to ourselves but we made the mistake of telling our plumber what we planned to do.

He turned out to be a direct descendant of Charles Marcel and he hasn't been back since. No one approves and we're not sure that we're going to get away with it. It does us no good to point out that there's been a revolution since Louis Quinze.

"That was Louis Seize," we are reminded.

Marcel has been sulking about the thing for days now, and when Marcel sulks everything is at a standstill. He told us that he once sulked for fifteen days, during which time he spoke to no one, including his wife. Even when Marcel isn't sulking he drinks five liters of wine a day. We think at least that we ought to be able to send Louis Quinze our liquor bill.

We don't know what we should do about Marcel because for one thing we're not sure we don't own him. He came with the house and may be attached to the land in some feudal fashion.

We've bought ourselves a crowbar and several splendid hammers but we simply haven't dared touch Louis Quinze. The electricians marched out in a body just yesterday. (They were afraid to disturb the *boiserie*.)

There hasn't been much summer anyway, and we've been thinking how nice it would be to stick in a radiator or two against the winter. Heaven only knows how Louis Quinze is going to feel about that.

Max Ernst

Originally published as "A Place on the Map: Arizonan Wins World Art Prize," *Evening Tribune* (San Diego, CA), Thursday, September 2, 1954

PARIS—We think it a shame that no one has sufficiently remarked the fact that for the first time in the history of the Venice Biennale the Grand Prize in painting was awarded to an American citizen. The reason for this may well be that most people forget to think of Max Ernst of Sedona, Ariz., as an American.

Max Ernst was born in Germany and made his early reputation as a painter. But assuming that it is always better to be chosen than to be taken for granted, we Americans should be especially appreciative of the honor he has reaped for his adopted country. In a sense he has put us on the art map.

The grand prize of the President of the Council of Ministers is the most important international painting prize and brings with it one and a half million lire. In addition, the City of Venice and the Gallery of Modern Art in Rome will each buy a painting from Max Ernst. In the last three years the prize has been won by Georges Braque, Henri Matisse, and Raoul Dufy, all of them French.

It was something of a surprise when Max Ernst won it this year. Most people thought the French would win again with Georges Rouault and the Spaniard, Joan Miró, was expected to be strong at the finish. Both are particularly in vogue and Max Ernst, besides being American, is a steadfast surrealist, popularly considered these days as old horse.

Anyway, our ambassador to Italy, Mrs. Claire Booth Luce, came from Rome for the inauguration and seemed quite pleased, according to Ernst, that such great recognition should be bestowed on a compatriot by the international jury.

We asked Max Ernst to tell us all about the Biennale, which he described as a must for anybody interested in the arts. Every artist who can manage it attends.

It is sort of a super-convention of the trade. Moreover it provides a bird's-eye view of the whole world of painting and sculpture as it is being made today.

There are thirty-three countries represented and roughly 650 artists. There is, of course, another main prize which goes to an Italian artist, inasmuch as Italy does not compete with the nations it has invited.

As its name would insist, the Biennale is a biannual art festival. It was established at the beginning of the century.

Since the war it has been the habit to adopt a theme selected by an international committee. The themes of last years have been cubism, futurism, and fauvism. This year the theme is surrealism.

Each country participating may select the artists it wishes to represent it, but, in addition, the Italian government invites its guests of honor, usually one or two painters and one or two sculptors.

This year the painters so honored were Max Ernst and Joan Miró, with the sculptor Hans Arp. Separate rooms were set aside for the exhibitions of these artists.

The festival is held in a large park on the edge of Venice two gondola stops from the Piazza San Marco. The park is furnished with permanent pavilions which, for the most part, have been set up by the participating nations.

It is a very luxurious setting and, according to Max Ernst, one of the only places in Venice where one sees trees.

We asked Mr. Ernst how he felt about winning the prize. What he felt best about, he said, was that it stood for a triumph of an art that has never received official recognition.

Recently there has been too much preoccupation with the textural and decorative in painting to the exclusion of real magic and content. A group representing the nations of the world recognize that something new is going on.

He added that he was encouraged that this should happen at a time when painting is becoming like wallpaper, a tendency which discourages spiritual adventure.

We had to ask him what he was planning to do with the money. He laughed and said it reminded him of another time he'd been interviewed. A magazine reporter had admired his Arizona studio but expressed the opinion that it might be improved by adding a roof.

The award has helped put Max Ernst in a position to take this advice.

Bettina Yonick

Originally published as "Blonde with Subtle Eyes: Opera Singer Fits a New Pattern," *Evening Tribune* (San Diego, CA), Thursday, December 9, 1954

Paris—Usually it is too bad to have one's illusions shattered. The world is a sadder place to live in after Santa Claus's beard comes off in one's hand or after one sees wrinkles in a real-life movie star. The world would be a sad place indeed, though, if this didn't work both ways, and if there weren't some reillusions to offset such disillusions.

Take opera singers, for instance. Through the years we have sadly come to accept them as huge ungainly creatures shrieking Wagner and knocking over stage sets. How could we be sympathetic when the sad young hero took his own life in the last act over a girl he couldn't have lifted over the threshold of a dream cottage if there'd been a happy ending?

We were expecting the inevitable when we met Bettina Yonick. We met her because she wanted to be at the station for the arrival of some friends of hers, who were coming to stay with us. Because it was such an ungodly hour in the morning and because we were expecting the inevitable we decided to arrive in a semi-somnambulant state and not to really wake up till sometime after lunch.

She'd promised to wear a purple chrysanthemum as identification and when we saw what the purple chrysanthemum was wearing we woke up in a hurry. We let our coffee get cold while we went on staring, for Miss Yonick is a blonde, with subtly changeable eyes, is twenty-six years old, stands five feet six, and weighs 128 pounds.

We learned that she'd become an opera singer quite by accident when she joined the Trojan Women's Glee Club at the University of Southern California to pick up an easy credit. Up to that time, she'd always thought she was going to be a ballet dancer, which we think must have been what saved her figure.

Since her graduation from college 1948 Miss Yonick has done nothing but sing. She first sang for the Civic Light Opera Company and then did five months on the road with *Oklahoma*, which she remembers rather vividly because she lost her petticoat during a certain performance which she rather thinks was in Cincinnati.

She made her opera debut with the Detroit Opera series, did a season with the Opera Nacional in Mexico, toured in *La Bohème*, and sang with the Charles Wagner Opera Company. She has been invited to give concerts at Columbia University and the Salzburg Festival.

We wanted to know to whom we should feel grateful for bringing her to Paris. For this she takes most of the credit herself. She had been invited back to Salzburg, which was understandable to us even though we hadn't heard her sing. At this point she decided to put all of her eggs in the same basket.

She feels that there is a much better chance for her here than in the States. Both the Metropolitan Opera and the New York City Center have a preference for European singers and there aren't enough opera houses in America to give everybody a chance. In Germany alone there are eighty-eight.

We offered Miss Yonick a cigarette, but she turned it down.

Then we asked her what operas she liked best to sing in. Her favorite is *Salome* because she likes the idea of singing for a head. Also she likes *Madama Butterfly* and *Rosenkavalier*. As a matter of fact she likes any opera that will give her a chance to act as well as to sing. She feels that opera is as much drama as it is music and we couldn't help thinking how much it would hurt us to have her waste away before our eyes in the last act of *Bohème*.

We asked her if she got invited to dinner often enough, and she sighed and looked a little melancholy as she might look in a certain scene from *Werther*. Opera singers have to keep on a high-protein diet and get a minimum of twelve hours sleep a night. "Who's going to buy a girl a steak if he has to take her home at 10 o'clock?" Also sometimes she has to go for days without talking.

Still we asked her if she wasn't going to stay around Paris for a while. No, she's off to Germany. We suggested that maybe she might get an offer to sing in Paris. She sighed again and looked sadder than Ophelia. She had turned down the only offer she'd had, which was a fat contract with the Folies Bergère.

Vernissages

Originally published as "Vernissage Popular: You Can Warm Up
and View Art, Too," *Evening Tribune* (San Diego, CA), Thursday,
January 27, 1955

PARIS—Now that winter has arrived, we're all going back to
vernissages with a vengeance. As any good Parisian knows,
vernissage comes from the French word *vernis*, meaning "varnish,"
and was originally the evening when a painter would invite all
his friends to help him varnish his pictures on the eve of the
opening of his exhibition. Theoretically, it is still considered
the eve of the opening, but, since it is the only time that anyone
ever comes into a gallery, it can be argued that the vernissage is
a one-night stand.

No artist who is worth his salt would consider having his
vernissage in anything but the most disagreeable weather, and
his importance as an artist is in direction proportion to how cold
it is when his show goes up. There is, of course, a reason for this,
as any unfortunate soul who winters here can tell you. It is out
of the question to stay home, as there is no heat.

Like our own American ancestors the only solution the French
have hit upon is bundling, only, being a garrulous race, they do
it in crowds. The human body does throw off a certain amount
of heat, and the clientele at the Deux Magots has a greater caloric
output than any central heating system yet devised in this otherwise most sympathetic country.

Except for certain disadvantages which we intended to discuss
hereunder, the vernissage provides an even better method of
huddling against the cold. For one thing, it costs absolutely nothing. For another thing, people pack better upright than in a seated

position. Furthermore, people have a tendency to dress up for vernissages, and often they bathe while they're about it.

On the other side of the ledger, there are the paintings and the artist to contend with. If you arrive early or it simply isn't cold enough, you find yourself virtually alone in the gallery. You are then obliged to stand before each painting for an absolute minimum of twenty seconds, knowing that at any instant you will be presented to the artist and expected to say something intelligent about each picture. For what it's worth, we're passing on what we have learned about what conduct to follow here.

The stance should be a comfortable one, feet close together with one knee slightly flexed. With the left hand, grip the right elbow tightly and lower your chin firmly into the palm of the right hand, being sure that the fingers are pressed tightly over the lips.

This is of utmost importance, as artists have the nasty habit of sneaking up behind you to try to hear what you are saying about their work. This position gives an impression of concentration and pensive interest. Avoid all gestures of approval or disapproval unless the show has already been reviewed and the coast is clear.

On being presented to the artist, one can congratulate him soundly, provided no one else is in hearing distance, but here again caution should be the rule. The words "very interesting" will never get you in any trouble you can't get out of provided they are uttered with no recognizable intonation.

Of course, if you are willing to sacrifice a little warmth and arrive properly late, you may not have to contend with the paintings at all except if they happen to be still wet and come off on the back of your suit. Generally they'll be screened by a wall of shoulders. Also under the right circumstances you may not have to meet the artist.

Nevertheless, we suggest that the pensive stance be strictly adhered to. The artist may be a friend of yours, but the chances are that you won't recognize him in a suit. Also, by covering the lower part of your face, you may avoid recognition by people you know but whose names you've forgotten.

With a little bit of what is known in these parts as "savoir faire," one can practicably get through the coldest winters just by attending vernissages. It sometimes happens, however, that the vernissage you're going to is your own. If this should be the case, let us recommend again the pensive stance. You will find out what everybody thinks about your work, and they will always find somebody else in a blue suit to congratulate.

Chronology

1919   Born January 24. Admitted to New York Foundling Hospital in Manhattan as an infant. Identity of biological parents unknown (access to hospital records restricted at time of publication).

1921   Adopted by utilities magnate and newspaper publisher Ira Clifton Copley, a congressman, and his wife, Edith Strohn Copley, of Aurora, Illinois. Named William Nelson Copley, the child is their second adoption, following James Strohn Copley, William's brother, adopted in 1917.

1921–29   Family resides in Aurora at 434 West Downer Place. Ira C. Copley incorporates Copley Press in 1928, purchasing the *San Diego Union* and *Evening Tribune*. Family relocates to San Diego, California. Edith Copley dies on October 25, 1929, as a result of complications from surgery.

1929–33   Attends Norton School in Claremont, California. Father remarries in 1931.

1933–38   Attends Phillips Academy in Andover, Massachusetts.

1938–41   Enters Yale University as an English major. Completes three years of study without graduating.

1941–44   Enlists in military while a junior at Yale. Inducted at Fort Sheridan, Illinois. Assigned to 62nd Coast Artillery in England. Later participates in campaigns in Algeria, French Morocco, Tunisia, and Rome.

1945   Returns to United States. *San Diego Union* publishes January 25 article on Copley's military service, mentioning his war novel manuscript. Receives Honorable Discharge in September. Marries Doris Wead, daughter of novelist and screenwriter Frank Wead, in Los Angeles, on September 15. Meets brother-in-law John Fraser McLeish, an artist, who works as an illustrator and voice actor for Disney. McLeish goes by the name John Ployardt. Ployardt introduces Copley to art and Surrealism.

1946   Begins painting. Birth of son, William Bryant Copley, November 19.

1947   Plans to open gallery with Ployardt. Copley and Ployardt introduce themselves to Man Ray at his studio on Vine Street. Ira C.

Copley dies November 2. Copley and brother James each receive 4/9 ownership stake in the Copley Press, which then controls twelve newspapers in Southern California and Illinois. Copley and Ployardt write to Walter Arensberg on December 15, requesting advice on starting a gallery.

1948   Copley and Ployardt travel to New York in March. They meet Marcel Duchamp, Alexander Iolas, Julien Levy, Joseph Cornell, and others. Shortly thereafter, they travel to Sedona, Arizona, to meet Max Ernst and Dorothea Tanning. Copley and Ployardt spend six weeks in Mexico. Birth of daughter Claire Strohn Copley, August 14.

1948–49   The Copley Galleries opens at 257 North Canon Drive, Beverly Hills, on September 9, with a show of paintings by René Magritte. Subsequent shows are one-person exhibitions by Joseph Cornell, Roberto Matta Echaurren, Yves Tanguy, Man Ray, and Max Ernst. Copley acquires artworks from each exhibition in order to maintain a sales guarantee, thus forming the beginning of his art collection. Financial concerns necessitate closure of gallery.

1949   Separates from Doris Wead. Travels to Paris in the summer to paint but returns to California after death of stepmother, Chloe Davidson Copley, on August 1. Begins relationship with Gloria de Herrera, a secretary for Los Angeles County Museum of Art curator James B. Byrnes, and friend of Man and Juliette Ray.

1950   Lives and works in converted firehouse in Hollywood. Copley and Wead divorce.

1951   Copley's first one-person show is held at Royer's Book Shop in Los Angeles, January 15–30. Rudiments of Copley's figurative narrative style are in evidence, alongside imagery he will revisit in later work. Travels to New York before leaving United States for Paris. Visits Katherine Dreier in Milford, Connecticut, with Marcel Duchamp; sees Duchamp's *Tu m'* and *The Bride Stripped Bare by Her Bachelors, Even*. March 15: voyage to Paris aboard SS *De Grasse* with Gloria de Herrera, and Man and Juliette Ray. In Paris, resides at 19 rue Rousselet.

1951–56   Writes newspaper articles as a foreign correspondent for the Copley Press, receiving an annual salary of $22,000.

1952   Begins painting in studio at Impasse Ronsin.

1953   First one-person show in Europe, at Galerie Nina Dausset, Paris.
        Candies with printed wrappers featuring a phrase by Duchamp
        (*A Guest + A Host = A Ghost*) are given out at the opening. Begins
        relationship with Noma Rathner. Known later as an artist and
        jeweler, Rathner is affiliated with art circles on the West Coast
        and in Europe. The couple is married on New Year's Eve in Paris.

1954   William and Noma honeymoon in Egypt. First one-person show
        in Italy, at Galeria Montenapoleone, Milan. Max Ernst contributes
        text to exhibition brochure. Purchases home in Longpont-sur-
        Orge at 27 rue du Darier. The house will be the couple's primary
        residence until 1963. In Chicago, the William and Noma Copley
        Foundation is formed to award grants for visual art and music.
        Board of Directors includes Marcel Duchamp, Darius Milhaud,
        and Barnet Hodes, an attorney and art collector. Among first to
        receive grants are Joseph Cornell and composer Benjamin Lees.

1954–70   William and Noma Copley Foundation (later renamed
        Cassandra Foundation) awards grants to a diverse group of
        artists and composers and, beginning in 1959, publishes a series
        of monographs on ten artists: René Magritte, Jacques Herold,
        Hans Bellmer, Richard Lindner, Bernard Pfriem, Serge
        Charchoune, James Metcalf, Thomas Skills, Dieter Roth, and
        Eduardo Paolozzi. Artist Richard Hamilton is retained to super-
        vise editing and production of the latter nine publications.

1955   Begins prolific series of paintings exploring images of cars and
        street scenes in complex, multilayered compositions. Cofinances
        new edition of Duchamp's *Box in a Valise*, assembled by Duchamp
        and publisher Iliazd in Paris. Files lawsuit against brother James
        S. Copley and the First National Bank of Chicago for mismanag-
        ing assets of the Ira C. Copley Estate.

1956   Series of car paintings debuts in one-person show at Galerie
        du Dragon in Paris. Work included in XII Salon de Mai at Musée
        d'Art Moderne de la Ville de Paris. In December, William and
        Noma travel to Los Angeles for Christmas, to spend time with
        Copley's two children, who join them for part of their extended
        vacation in Mexico City.

1957   Paints while in Mexico. In April, hosts Marcel Duchamp in
        Mexico City. Travels to Chicago, where a lawsuit settlement is
        reached. The agreement permits James S. Copley to purchase

Copley's remaining stock in the Copley Press for $11.8 million. Returns to Europe. Intense period of painting. New works incorporate silhouetted images, extensive patterning, and small, cartoonlike renderings of nude women, bowler-hatted men, dachshunds, and policemen.

1958 Returns to Mexico, where he paints in advance of forthcoming exhibition in New York. Works in Diego Rivera's former studio at the home of collector and patron Dolores Olmedo in Acapulco. First exhibition in New York, at Alexander Iolas Gallery. Iolas becomes Copley's primary dealer for the next two decades. Agrees to cofinance production of Robert Lebel's monograph on Marcel Duchamp, *Sur Marcel Duchamp*.

1959 Gives opening remarks at Man Ray's exhibition at ICA, London, April 2. One-person show at Galerie Furstenberg, Paris. The show's success is marked by strong sales (sixteen paintings) and positive reviews. Editions Trianon releases *Sur Marcel Duchamp*. The British and American editions include Copley's translation of text by Henri-Pierre Roché. Group shows include two in Paris: XV Salon de Mai at Musée d'Art Moderne de La Ville de Paris and *Exposition inteRnatiOnale du Surréalisme* at Galerie Daniel Cordier.

1960 A period of sobriety. One-person shows at Gallerina d'Arte Naviglio, Milan, and Gallerina del Cavallino, Venice.

1961 One-person shows at Alexander Iolas Gallery, New York, and Institute of Contemporary Arts, London. Copley's studio in Longpont, designed by architects Jane Drew and Maxwell Fry, is completed. Lends significant number of works for *Surréalisme et précurseurs* at Palais Granvell, Besançon, France. Begins series of satirical flag-themed paintings and textile works.

1962 One-person shows at Galleria Schwarz, Milan, and Galerie Iris Clert, Paris, where he presents works from the *Flags* series. William and Noma prepare to return to the United States permanently, deciding to move to New York in the winter. Group shows include XVIIII Salon de Mai at Musée d'Art Moderne de La Ville de Paris and *Collage Out of California* at Pasadena Art Museum. Copley's assemblage in the Pasadena show, incorporating a syringe, is confiscated by the Health Department.

1963 Moves to New York. Rents townhouse at 143 E. 69th Street before

moving into nearby apartment at 150 E. 69th Street. Both resi-
dences are located on the same street as the New York Foundling
Hospital where he was adopted in 1921. First studio in New York
located in SoHo near Broadway and Bond Street. One-person
shows at Hanover Gallery, London; Galerie Iris Clert, Paris; and
Alexander Iolas Gallery, New York. Group shows include 18 Salon
de réalités nouvelles at Musée Municipal d'Art Moderne, Paris,
XIX Salon de Mai, Musée d'Art Moderne de La Ville de Paris, and
Pop Art USA at Oakland Museum of Art. "Man Ray: The Dada
of Us All" is published in *Art News*.

1964   One-person show at David Stuart Gallery, Los Angeles. Marcia
Tucker, later curator, and founder of the New Museum, is hired
by Copley to assist with planning for his museum retrospective
at Stedelijk Museum Amsterdam scheduled for 1966.

1965–96   Participates in numerous group shows in Europe and the
United States.

1965   One-person shows in Chicago; Chula Vista, California; and
Houston, Texas. Publishes two artist's books, both titled *The Evil
I . . . or The Story of My Life*. Richard Hamilton assists with
production. Museum of Modern Art acquires its first work by
Copley, *Think* (1964). Begins series of monochrome-style
paintings employing dashed contour lines and areas of raw,
unprimed canvas.

1966   One-person show at Alexander Iolas Gallery, New York, titled
Projects for Monuments to the Unknown Whore. Later revisits the
exhibition's themes in a 1986 installation at the New Museum.
First European retrospective at the Stedelijk Museum Amsterdam.
Opening is attended by Man Ray, René Magritte, Max Ernst,
and Marcel Duchamp, who pose for a group photograph. In
New York, Copley sees *Étant donnés* at Duchamp's E. 11th Street
studio; agrees to acquire it through the Cassandra Foundation on
condition it be donated to the Philadelphia Museum of Art.
Begins series of paintings inspired by lyrics of American ballads
and folk songs.

1967   Works from new series are presented in two one-person shows:
Ballads at Galerie Iolas, Paris, and *Homage to Robert W. Service* at
Alexander Iolas Gallery, New York. William and Noma separate,
divorcing in 1968. One-person show of drawings at Bodley

Gallery, New York. Begins planning, with artist Dmitri Petrov, a new publication venture called The Letter Edged in Black Press, Inc., which will publish *S.M.S.*, an artists' magazine.

1968 Hiatus from painting. Six issues of *S.M.S.* are published, each of which contains a portfolio of facsimile multiples by artists, writers, and composers. Marcel Duchamp dies October 2 in Neuilly-sur-Seine, France. "Marcel Duchamp 1887–1968" published in the *New York Times*. Copley begins relationship with Stella Yang, a novelist (writing as Chuang Hua); they are married and move into an apartment on 81st Street and Central Park West.

1969 Installation and exhibition of *Étant donnés* at Philadelphia Museum of Art. "The New Piece" published in *Art in America*. Purchases home in Roxbury, Connecticut. Death of John Ployardt in automobile accident. Resumes painting. One-person show in Venice.

1970 One-person shows at Alexander Iolas Gallery, New York; Galerie Springer, Berlin; Galerie Neundorf, Cologne; and David Stuart Gallery, Los Angeles. Studio located at 33 W. 67th Street. Museum of Modern Art acquires *Marché commun (The Common Market)* (1961). Three-person show *Copley, Brauner & Magritte* at Louisiana Gallery, Houston. Begins new series of paintings and drawings of loosely rendered items from vintage Sears Roebuck catalogs set against bold, colorful background patterns.

1971 Presents *Nouns* series in one-person show at Alexander Iolas Gallery, New York.

1972 Birth of daughter Theodora Yang Copley, February 13. One-person show, *Mail Order*, at Alexander Iolas Gallery, New York. Participates in Documenta 5 in Kassel, Germany, curated by Harald Szeemann; eight (of ten) artworks are stolen. Verlag Gebr. König publishes artist's book *Notes on a Project for a Dictionary of Ridiculous Images*. Begins ambitious new series of paintings and charcoal drawings based on images from adult magazines.

1973 James S. Copley dies October 17. Claire Copley opens Claire S. Copley Gallery in Los Angeles. One-person show in Italy. Two works from new series, *X-Rated*, are included in *Erotic Art*, Art Center of the New School for Social Research, New York.

1974 Debuts paintings and works on paper from *X-Rated* series in large one-person show at New York Cultural Center. Exhibition catalog published with interview by Sam Hunter. German collector and gallerist Reinhard Onnasch presents two one-person shows of Copley's work: *Bill Copley: 1948–1972*, at Onnasch Galerie, New York, a career survey that travels to Moore College of Art, Philadelphia, and *Western Songs*, presenting works from the *Ballads* series, at Onnasch Galerie, Cologne. Completes text for "Portrait of the Artist as a Young Dealer" around this time, distributing undated typescripts to friends and colleagues.

1975   One-person show in Nantucket. Begins series of bicentennial-themed works based on American history tropes. Completes text for "About the Hare and the Tortoise but Mostly About the Hare" around this time.

1976   Bicentennial-themed exhibition *The Patriotism of CPLY: 1776 and All That* at Alexander Iolas Gallery, New York. Exhibition is mounted in slightly different form at David Stuart Gallery, Los Angeles. "Joseph Cornell" published in *Joseph Cornell Portfolio*.

1977   First one-person show at Phyllis Kind Gallery, Chicago. Separates from Stella Yang Copley. Purchases apartment at 52 E. 89th Street. "Portrait" is published in French translation in *Paris–New York*. A cover design by Copley is used for the exhibition's companion publication, *Paris–New York: un album*. With assistant Edwin Helmsley, creates a suite of eight wall-hanging mirror artworks, based on earlier paintings. With artist and filmmaker Viola Stephan, coauthors play, *Even If You're Unhappy Is No Reason Why You Shouldn't Behave Yourself*, which is staged at Brooks Jackson Gallery Iolas, New York.

1978   Mirror works presented in one-person show *The Temptation of St. Anthony* at Brooks Jackson Gallery Iolas. One-person shows at Galerie Springer, Berlin; Galerie Rudolf Zwirner, Cologne; and Galerie Fassbender, Munich. Group shows include *"Bad" Painting*, New Museum, New York, curated by Marcia Tucker. Begins series of paintings based on Francis Picabia's *La Nuit espagnole* (1922), which Copley acquired in 1956 and sold in 1975 to collector Peter Ludwig.

1979   Picabia series is presented in one-person show *Variations on a Theme by Francis Picabia* at Brooks Jackson Gallery Iolas. The show is subsequently presented at David Stuart Gallery, Los

Angeles. Produces and publishes artist's calendar based on the series. In Houston, Rice University presents *Reflection on a Past Life*, a retrospective drawn from Houston collections. Exhibition catalogue includes first English publication of "Portrait of the Artist as a Young Dealer." Major sale of works from Copley's collection at Sotheby Parke-Bernet, November 5–6, sets numerous sales records. Among the lots is Man Ray's *Observatory Time, the Lovers*, 1932–34, which sells for $750,000. Copley and Stella Yang are divorced.

1980   One-person show *Whorses* at Brooks Jackson Gallery Iolas. Marries Marjorie Annapav, September 15, in Roxbury, Connecticut. Marriage party held at Copley's 89th Street apartment two weeks later. Comprehensive retrospective opens at Kunsthalle Bern, Switzerland, in October. Curated by Johannes Gachnang, the exhibition travels to Musée National d'Art Moderne, Centre Pompidou, Paris; Stedelijk Van Abbemuseum, Eindhoven; and Badischer Kunstverein, Karlsruhe. Included in two group shows at the Whitney Museum of American Art.

1981   In January, injured during fire at his Key West residence. Separation and divorce from Marjorie Annapav. One-person show *Retrocplytive* at Brooks Jackson Gallery, New York; other one-person shows at Lens Fine Art, Anvers, Belgium, and Galerie Klewan, Munich. Group shows include *Westkunst*, Museen Der Stadt Köln, Cologne.

1982   One-person shows in New York, Chicago, and Munich. Death of H. C. Westermann; places full-page remembrance in *Artforum*. Paints series of paravents, or screens. Included in Documenta 7, Kassel.

1983   One-person show at Phyllis Kind Gallery, New York, of screens and new work that revisits imagery from earlier cars series. Filmed interview with Phyllis Kind appears on Episode 8 of *Andy Warhol's TV*, aired on Manhattan Cable TV. One-person show *Post-Raphaelite Paintings* at Onnasch Galerie, Berlin.

1984   Included in group exhibition *Paravents*, Schloss-Lörsfeld, Kerpen, Germany.

1985   One-person show *Acopleyshments: 1955–1985* at Phyllis Kind Gallery; other one-person shows at Quay Gallery, San Francisco, and Galerie Susanna Kulli, Zurich.

1986   New Museum presents *Tomb of the Unknown Whore*, an exhibition and installation conceived by Copley. Visitors to the exhibition are provided with chalk and encouraged to write on the paintings and walls.

1987   Undergoes coronary bypass surgery. Sends notes for a planned lecture, "In My Career as a Name-Dropper," to Anne d'Harnoncourt. One-person shows at Galerie Kewenig, Frechen-Bachem, Germany, and Phyllis Kind Gallery, New York.

1988   Marries Jackie Prescott, a doctor, on March 27, at Grand Bay Hotel, Florida. One-person show at Galerie 1900–2000, Paris.

1989   Copley and Prescott divorce. One-person show at Phyllis Kind Gallery, Chicago.

1990   First German edition of "Portrait of the Artist as a Young Dealer" published by Gachnang & Springer. One-person show at Galerie Klewan, Munich.

1991   One-person show, *CPLY: Trust Lust Heed Greed*, presented at Phyllis Kind Gallery's New York and Chicago spaces. Completes prolific series of works on paper. *Paintings and Drawings 1951–1991* at David Nolan Gallery, New York; other one-person shows at Galerie Fred Jahn, Stuttgart, and Galleria Peccolo, Livorno.

1992   Moves to Sugarloaf Key, Florida. Marries Cynthia Gooch, a resident of Key West. One-person shows in Milan and Munich.

1993   One-person show at Galleria Zell Am See, Schloss Rosenberg, Austria. Group shows include *Berliner Amerikaner*, Haus Am Lutzoplatz, Berlin, for which an artist's book, *Techniques of Fornication*, is published in a three-volume set with books by Dorothy Iannone and Emmett Williams. On November 8, Christie's New York presents a sale featuring contemporary artworks from Copley's collection.

1994   One-person shows at Nolan/Eckman Gallery, New York; Galerie Klewan, Munich; and Galerie Heike Curtze, Vienna. Group shows include *Old Glory: The American Flag in Contemporary Art*, Cleveland Center for Contemporary Art.

1995   Retrospective *William N. Copley: Heed Greed Trust Lust* presented at Kestner-Gesselschaft, Hanover. One-person shows in Zurich, Heidelberg, and Cologne. Verlag Walther König publishes artist's book *The Strumpet Muse: Images from Robert W. Service*.

1996   One-person shows at Nolan/Eckman Gallery, New York, and

Galerie Fred Jahn, Munich. Group shows include *A Labor of Love*, New Museum, New York. In early May, Copley suffers a series of strokes in Sugarloaf Key. He dies on May 7.

Sources

Claire Brandon, "Chronology," *William N. Copley*, ed. Germano Celant (Milan: Fondazione Prada; Houston, TX: Menil Collection, 2016), 42–48, 74–145, 172–303.

William N. Copley, Correspondence and Archival Records (1947–96), CPLY Archives, William N. Copley Estate, New York.

Paul B. Franklin, "'A Guest + A Host = A Ghost': The Friendship and Collaborations of Marcel Duchamp and William N. Copley," *William N. Copley*, ed. Germano Celant (Milan: Fondazione Prada; Houston, TX: Menil Collection, 2016), 58–71.

Michael Taylor, *Marcel Duchamp: Étant donnés* (Philadelphia, PA: Philadelphia Museum of Art; New Haven, CT: Yale University Press), 129–35.

Deborah Treisman and Anne Doran, *The Dream Colony: A Life in Art* (New York: Bloomsbury, 2017), 154.

Note on the Texts

I. Writings About Art and Artists

Address by William N. Copley, Esq.
Typescript dated April 2, 1959. Previously unpublished.
CPLY Archives, William N. Copley Estate, New York.

Serge Charchoune
First published as "Introducing the Paintings of Serge Charchoune"
Art News 59 (March 1960), 34–36, 55–56; reprinted in Richard
Hamilton, ed., *Charchoune* (Chicago, IL: William and Noma Copley
Foundation, 1963), n.p. Reprint reproduced in this volume.

Man Ray: The Dada of Us All
First published in *Portfolio*, no. 7 (Winter 1963), 14–23, 111–13;
reprinted in William Copley and Janus, *Man Ray: Inventor/Painter/Poet*
(New York: New York Cultural Center, 1974): n.p. Reprint reproduced
in this volume.

Marcel Duchamp 1887–1968
Originally published as "Marcel Duchamp 1887–1968," *New York
Times*, October 13, 1968, D37.

The New Piece
Originally published as "The New Piece," *Art in America* 57, no. 4
(July–August 1969): 36.

Portrait of the Artist as a Young Dealer
Copley's original typescripts (titled "Portrait of the Artist as a
Young Art Dealer") are undated; however, mailed copies suggest
the text was completed as early as October 1974. The memoir
was first published in French translation as "Portrait de l'artiste
en jeune marchand de tableaux" in *Paris–New York* (Paris: Centre
Georges Pompidou, 1977), 135–62. It was first published in

English in *CPLY: Reflection on a Past Life* (Houston, TX: Institute for the Arts, Rice University, 1979), 5–35. Latter text reprinted in this volume.

About the Hare and the Tortoise but Mostly About the Hare
First published in French translation by Carolyn Breakspear as "Du lièvre et de la tortue et principalement du lièvre" in Jean-Hubert Martin and Hélène Seckel, eds., *Francis Picabia* (Paris: Galeries Nationales du Grand Palais, 1976), 13–18. Author's typescript reproduced in this volume. Though undated, the text was likely completed in 1975, prior to the Francis Picabia exhibition at the Galeries Nationales du Grand Palais from January 23 to March 29, 1976.

Joseph Cornell
Originally published in *Joseph Cornell Portfolio* (New York: Leo Castelli Gallery; New York: Richard L. Feigen and Company; New York/Los Angeles: James Corcoran Gallery, 1976), n.p.

In My Career as a Name-Dropper
Letter to Anne d'Harnoncourt, dated November 4, 1987, with notes for a planned talk on the occasion of *Apropos of Marcel Duchamp 1887/1987* (Philadelphia Museum of Art, October 1, 1987–January 3, 1988). Marcel Duchamp Exhibition Records, Series VI, Subseries A, Box 25, Folder 13, Philadelphia Museum of Art, Library and Archives.

II. Interviews, Texts, and Letters

Excerpts from Oral History Interview with William Nelson Copley
Excerpts taken from corrected transcript held by William N. Copley Estate. Although the transcript carries a date of January 30, 1968, the topics covered in the interview suggest that it was conducted in 1969. For a full transcript, see Paul Cummings, "Oral history interview with William Nelson Copley, 1968 January 30," Archives of American Art, Smithsonian Institution, accessed September 8, 2019, https://www.aaa.si.edu/collections/interviews/oral-history-interview-william-nelson-copley-12646.

Project for a Dictionary of Platitudes
Originally published in *CPLY* (New York: Alexander Iolas Gallery, 1970), n.p.

CPLY: An Interview by Sam Hunter
Originally published as "CPLY: An Interview by Sam Hunter," in *CPLY: X-Rated* (New York: New York Cultural Center, 1974), n.p.

CPLY by Vincent Fremont
Originally published as "CPLY by Vincent Fremont," *Andy Warhol's Interview* VI, no. 2 (February 1976): 38.

Advice to a Young Artist
Letters from William N. Copley to artist Anne Doran. Published posthumously, with an introduction by Doran, in *CPLY 1919–1996: The Art of William Copley* (St. Louis, MO: Forum for Contemporary Art), 4–9.

Letter to Judith Young-Mallin
Handwritten letter. Previously unpublished. Judith Young-Mallin's correspondence with Copley involved discussions of a draft manuscript of Young-Mallin's history of the American Surrealists. A chapter in the manuscript focuses on the Copley Galleries and Copley's departure for France in 1951. Box 3, Folder 7, Young-Mallin Archives, Philadelphia Museum of Art, Library and Archives.

A Conversation with William Copley by Alan Jones
Originally published as "A Conversation with William Copley," *CPLY: William N. Copley* (New York: David Nolan Gallery, 1991), 5–15.

III. Early Writings

Copley Galleries to Show Works of Joseph Cornell
Originally published as "Copley Galleries to Show Works of Joseph Cornell," *San Diego Union*, September 26, 1948, 7-D. No author byline; attribution to Copley inferred by the writer's descriptive language and the publishing context.

Picasso
: Originally published as "Has Time to Be Human: Far-Famed Artist Greets Travelers," *San Diego Union*, July 1, 1951, A-3.

French Newspapers
: Originally published as "American in Paris: Reading Newspapers Chore for Tourists in France," *Daily News-Post* (Monrovia, CA), August 30, 1951, 5. Source reprinted in this volume published in unidentified newspaper as "French Newspapers." Scrapbook of Copley articles and manuscripts, Box 57, Young-Mallin Archive, Philadelphia Museum of Art, Library and Archives.

British Broadcasting Corp.
: Originally published as "English Too Good: Near Miss Scored with Radio Debut," *Evening Tribune* (San Diego, CA), April 23, 1952, B-3. Title supplied by editor. Box 57, Young-Mallin Archive.

Brancusi
: Originally published as "Living Close to Fame: Brancusi Buddy of Writer—Almost," *Daily News-Post* (Monrovia, CA), May 31, 1952, 3. Source reprinted in this volume published as "Close to Fame: Brancusi Buddy of Writer—Almost," *Glendale News Press*. Not dated but likely May 1952. Box 57, Young-Mallin Archive.

Leaving Paris
: Originally published as "Leaving an Effort: France Outside of Paris Discovered on Tour," *Daily News-Post* (Monrovia, CA), June 10, 1952, 14. Source reprinted in this volume published as "Copley Goes Touring: Discovers France Outside of Paris," *Daily Bank Review*. Not dated but likely June 1952. Box 57, Young-Mallin Archive.

Crime Passionnel
: Originally published as "Good Show: Murder Trial in France Proves Entertaining Affair," *Illinois State Journal*, December 15, 1952. Box 57, Young-Mallin Archive.

Billy Beck
: Originally published as "GI Gets New Identity," *Elgin (Illinois) Daily*

Courier-News, February 26, 1953, Box 57, 16. Young-Mallin Archive.

Antiquities
Originally published as "Ancient Tombs Numerous: Egypt
Antiquities Need Much Study," *Herald-News* (Joliet, Illinois),
April 6, 1954, 8. Title for this and following pieces derived from
Noma Copley, handwritten list of article titles, n.d., unless
noted. William N. Copley, Scrapbook No. 2, CPLY Archives,
William N. Copley Estate, New York.

House in the Country
Originally published as "Dream of Every Frenchman: Restoration
of House Baffling," *Daily News-Post* (Monrovia, CA), August 7,
1954, 5. Source reprinted in this volume published in unidentified
newspaper as "What About Marcel? House in the Country Everyone's
Dream," July 30, 1954. Title supplied by editor. Scrapbook No. 2,
CPLY Archives.

Max Ernst
Originally published as "A Place on the Map: Arizonan Wins World
Art Prize," *Evening Tribune* (San Diego, CA), September 2, 1954, A-20.
Scrapbook No. 2, CPLY Archives.

Bettina Yonick
Originally published as "Blonde with Subtle Eyes: Opera Singer Fits
a New Pattern," *Evening Tribune* (San Diego, CA), December 9, 1954,
A-15. Scrapbook No. 2, CPLY Archives.

Vernissages
Originally published as "Vernissage Popular: You Can Warm Up and
View Art, Too," *Evening Tribune* (San Diego, CA), January 27, 1955,
A-16. Scrapbook No. 2, CPLY Archives.

Chronology by Anthony Atlas

Cover — William N. Copley, c. 1964
Photograph by Nathan Rabin
Image courtesy William N. Copley Estate, New York

10–11 — Man Ray and William N. Copley, c. 1950
Photograph by Gloria de Herrera
© Estate of James Byrnes, Los Angeles

12 — Portrait of William N. Copley by Man Ray
© Man Ray 2015 Trust / Artists Rights Society (ARS), NY / ADAGP, Paris 2020

124–25 — William N. Copley in Paris, c. 1951
Photograph by Mike de Dulmen
Image courtesy William N. Copley Estate, New York

126 — Installation view: William N. Copley, *Tomb of the Unknown Whore*, New Museum, 1986
Photograph by Nathan Rabin
Image courtesy William N. Copley Estate, New York

198–99 — Copley Galleries, 257 North Canon Drive, Beverly Hills, c. 1948–49
Image courtesy William N. Copley Estate, New York

200 — William N. Copley, Noma Copley, and unidentified man, Egypt, c. January 1954
Image courtesy William N. Copley Estate, New York

Special thanks:
Valentina Branchini and David Nolan Gallery, Rose Chiango and Philadelphia Museum of Art Library and Archives, Anne Doran, Andrea Fisher-Scherer and Artists Rights Society, Max Hetzler and Galerie Max Hetzler, Judith Irrgang and Museum Frieder Burda, Mark Matchak, Susan Miller, Dan Nadel, Stephanie Seidel and ICA Miami.

Text set in Dante, designed by Giovanni Mardersteig in 1957.

About the editor:
Anthony Atlas is an archivist and independent curator based in New York.